The New York Times

WEEKEND WIZARD CROSSWORDS

The New York Times

WEEKEND WIZARD CROSSWORDS
50 Saturday and Sunday Puzzles

Edited by Will Shortz

ST. MARTIN'S GRIFFIN ⚑ NEW YORK

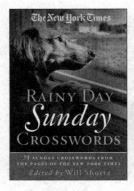
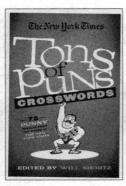

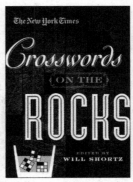

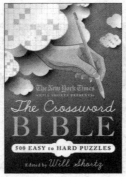
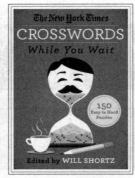

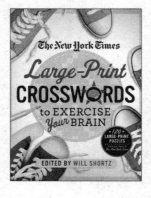

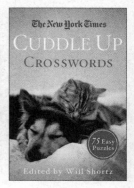

ACROSS

1 Bollix
6 Rough selection?
15 1975 Golden Globe winner
16 Merry Men member
17 Marty Robbins's "__ the Lucky One"
18 One doing 40+?
19 Speech closing?
20 They're laid down in shipyards
22 Notice after the expiration date?
23 "Uh, yeah!"
25 __ Rebellion (colonial uprising)
27 Just for Men target
28 Incidentally
31 Auntie Mame's secretary
33 Rear of a disco?
34 "__ Jeunes de Paris" (recurring "S.N.L." sketch)
37 Munchie often dipped in marinara
40 Info for air traffic control
41 Like some carpets and autumn leaves
42 Classic Harlem ballroom, with "the"
43 Feature of many a convertible or Jeep
45 Hinge
46 "The Return of Doctor X" star, 1939
49 Poet Howard who wrote "A Primer of the Daily Round"
51 Aéroports de Paris manages it
52 Kofi Annan's home
54 Before now
55 Ball carriers
58 Completely fixed
60 Its last model was the 1941 Skylark
61 Dean's "East of Eden" role
62 Eschewing a higher calling?
63 Maker of iComfort

DOWN

1 Crossword, e.g.
2 "Oops, that had escaped me"
3 Boxer-turned-sitcom star
4 Setting for Twins games: Abbr.
5 Traditional three-liner
6 Ejection protection
7 Month in which Creation began, by tradition
8 Triple-time dance, in Durango
9 Size up?: Abbr.
10 Phillie foe
11 Senselessness
12 No wuss
13 Liquid part of fat
14 "Shoot!"
21 Leave shore, perhaps
24 Cry for attention
25 Test letter?
26 It's unfathomable
29 Flat sign
30 "Whoa, whoa!"
32 Taste
34 Real-time storm tracker
35 One concerned with invasive species
36 Liquor with the slogan "West of Expected"
38 Major fault
39 Something discounted at a deli?
43 Argument-ending declaration
44 One with a signature role?
46 De Klerk succeeded him
47 "In __?"
48 Rosetta Stone figure
50 Trading places
52 Clench
53 Start to ski?
56 "Vous," informally
57 Special delivery figs.?
59 Ahead of, once

by Sam Ezersky

ACROSS

1 The "1" of 1/4
4 Org. portrayed in "American Hustle"
7 Conceal, in a way
11 Aloof
17 Subj. that gets into circulation?
19 Caterer's container
20 Starters
22 Spring
23 Greeting at the door
25 Daily newspaper feature, informally
26 Rabelaisian
27 Signs from above
28 Part of U.N.C.F.
30 "Nobody's infallible, not even me"
32 Literary genre of "David Copperfield" or "Ender's Game"
34 World-weary
35 U.K. record label
37 States
38 So-called "herb of remembrance"
40 Jimmy
43 Serenader, maybe
45 Something a chair has
47 "Candid Camera" feature
48 To the same extent
51 What a hippie lives in?
54 Takes to court
56 Novelist Frank who wrote "The Octopus"
58 She, in Brazil
59 Hipster beer, for short
61 Most IRT lines in the Bronx, e.g.
62 Cry of discovery
63 ____ cotta
65 Like smoothie fruit
67 Rocker Weymouth of the Talking Heads
71 Title song question in Disney's "Frozen"
75 ____ jacket
76 Abalone
77 Southern African desert
78 You can bank on it
79 Bygone French coin
81 Foreign policy grp.
82 Window units, briefly
83 ____ Stark, Oona Chaplin's "Game of Thrones" role
85 Friend's couch, perhaps
89 Stuffed Jewish dish
92 Leslie of "Gigi" and "Lili"
93 Singer Mann
94 "Tom ____" (#1 Kingston Trio hit)
96 Reclined
98 Sang like Ella
100 What may eat you out of house and home?
103 Hon
107 37-Across, informally
108 Some police attire
110 Academy Award winner who has played both a U.S. president and God
112 Cover subject on Ms. magazine's debut issue, 1972
115 Easily bribed
116 City burned in Genesis
117 ____ algebra
118 Scope
120 1990s craze
122 Eats up
123 Kitchen gadget
124 Free ad, for short
125 Water carrier
126 See 52-Down
127 Like stereotypical TV neighbors
128 Application info: Abbr.
129 Spanish article

DOWN

1 Pioneering urbanologist Jane
2 Inability to recall the names of everyday objects
3 To wit
4 Entertainment
5 Elicit
6 "Delaware Water Gap" painter George
7 Long period of stability ending circa A.D. 180
8 Part of Lawrence Welk's introduction
9 Enthusiastic, sociable, confident type, it's said
10 Norma Jean, later
11 Kitchen gadget
12 Certain weanling
13 One of a Greek trio
14 100% guaranteed
15 "Kinderszenen" composer
16 Exclamation repeated in the Monkees' TV theme song
18 Is a mixologist
21 Drug also known as Ecstasy
24 Big Ten rival of UMich
29 College sr.'s test
31 Award for Hunt and Peck
33 Shooters' org.
34 Its drafts may be crafts
36 Bothers
39 Fourth word in the "Star Wars" prologue
41 Kind of blue
42 Ones holding hands?
44 "Un Ballo in Maschera" aria
46 Hesitant start to a question
48 + end
49 "Ooh-la-la!"
50 Cold treat, informally
52 With 126-Across, first European to cross the Mississippi
53 Thrills
55 Website billed as "the front page of the Internet"
57 Clinches
60 Repast for a late riser
64 Singer Carly ____ Jepsen
65 ____ favor
66 Good wood for cabinetmaking
68 Where bombs are bursting, per Francis Scott Key
69 "Au contraire!"
70 "Gimme a break!"
72 Quick round of tennis
73 Takes on
74 Summers of old?
80 President Arthur's nickname
82 Feature of much modern architecture
84 Hill or dale
85 Mama ____
86 Popular Eastern beverage
87 Largest state of Brazil
88 Deadly viper
90 Suffix with hotel
91 Container in a 34-Down
95 Place to kick your feet up
97 Solid rock center?
99 Very much
101 ____ thruster (NASA system)
102 Wanders (around)
104 Traveling around the holidays, maybe
105 New Jersey town next to Fort Lee
106 1960s–'80s Pontiac
109 Substitute
111 Edward Snowden subj.
113 "Quo Vadis" character
114 Nutty
115 Tries to win
117 You can trip on it
119 Dude
121 Has the ability to

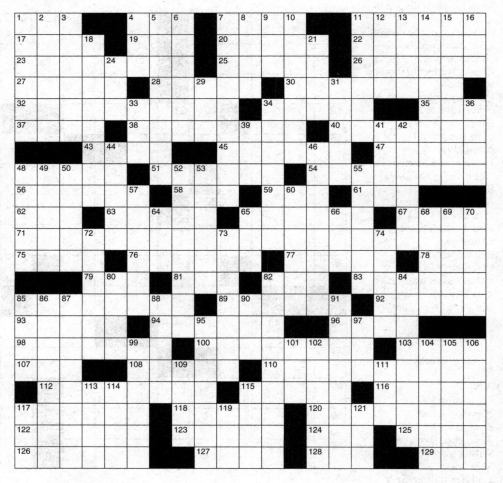

by Finn Vigeland

ACROSS

1 Subs' subs
7 "My old lady"
13 Many a Bedouin
15 Cigar with both ends open
16 Wraps around an island?
17 City across the Rio Grande from McAllen, Tex.
18 What may precede itself
19 Lover of Mattie in an Edith Wharton novel
21 Sulk
22 Flue flake
23 Mocha alternative
25 Souvenir sometimes made with shells
26 Vocalist's warm-up run
27 Gathering of stockholders?
28 L.A. law notable, once
29 Scorer of the first double eagle in U.S. Open history, 1985
31 "The Internship" co-star, 2013
33 "Really?"
34 Celsius, for one
38 The other side
39 Noted preschool sequence?
41 Question of introspection
42 Four at the fore?
43 Dolphin facility
44 Fizzler
45 Ugly __
46 It's west of James Bay: Abbr.
47 Adrenaline, informally
49 Drug delivery options, briefly
51 Important union members?
52 Guarantor of financial accounts, for short
54 How a champagne bottle may arrive
56 Natural thing to feel
57 Locale of five major U.S. volcanoes
60 Big wave, e.g.
61 Takes a breather

8 Common 60-Across
9 Shoreline avifauna
10 Masterpiece designated "quasi una fantasia"
11 Per a 1942 song, "She's making history, working for victory"
12 Radio heads
14 Many an old red giant
15 Packing option
20 Tucked away
23 Revolutionary figure
24 Thick plank insert?
30 Early Chinese dynasty
32 Trojans' foes
35 Joining the fray
36 Dingo dodger
37 Frenchy portrayer in "Grease"
40 What might be grabbed in a rush
42 Profs' backups
48 One with patches

50 Settle a score, old-style
53 Lemon who played for the 1984 World Series-winning Tigers
55 Langston Hughes poem with the lines "Nobody'll dare / Say to me, / 'Eat in the kitchen,' / Then"
56 Good name for a chauffeur?
58 Lead-__
59 French possessive

DOWN

1 Fighting losses
2 Invoice information
3 Water cycle studiers, e.g.
4 "Pink-__" (1966 Pink Panther short)
5 One of two extremes: Abbr.
6 Nevadans
7 "Such gall!"

by Joe Krozel

ACROSS

1 "Aladdin" antagonist
6 "___ God of hosts, hear my prayer"
11 Beam splitter
16 Face an ace
19 Historic time
20 People of Kenya
21 Powerball, for one
22 Uganda's Amin
23 The makeup affected the appearance of all the cast of "Casino," including ___
25 Guilty ___
26 Bit of evasive maneuvering
27 Singer Nina
28 "Think different," e.g.
30 Mentored one
32 Op-___
33 Court figs.
35 After the 1946 World Series, the dugout was filled with the Cardinals and their happy sounds, including ___
37 Wash
39 Card a 72, maybe
40 Son of Isaac
43 Ice dam sites
46 Grade school subj.
47 Whimpers
51 She said that when it comes to '60s teen idols, all you need to know is one thing: ___
54 Doll house?
56 One might be made over a beer
57 Dawn goddess
58 Allen's successor on late-night TV
60 2008 Obama catchword
61 Break up, as concrete
62 Opa-___, Fla.
64 Early Mexican
66 Headed up
67 The bartender poured beers for all the action movie stars, including ___
71 I.M. sent to a construction site?
73 Co-founder of the Black Panthers
74 "Star Trek" crew member
75 Bedouin
78 ___ Lee, singer with the 2011 #1 album "Mission Bell"
80 "And giving ___, up the chimney he rose"
81 French bloom
82 Complete
83 SAT needs
85 The members of the Metropolitan Opera were hit with a host of problems, including ___
88 Cause for an insurer's denial, maybe
89 It's east of S.A.
91 Schwarzenegger, informally
92 "Enough, I get it!"
93 Prior listings?
97 C. S. Lewis's lion
99 At Thanksgiving the Indians were impressed with the Pilgrims and their earth-toned platters, especially ___
104 Quarry, e.g.
105 Hundred Acre Wood denizen
108 Backdrop for many Bond films
109 More recent
111 Wows
113 Market initials in a red oval
114 Justice Kagan
116 While trading barbs during the filming of "M*A*S*H," no one was able to match ___
118 Game of logic
119 With full force
120 Form a secret union?
121 Battier of the N.B.A.
122 Cookie-selling org.
123 Showed some disapproval
124 Like a neutron star
125 Radioer's "T"

DOWN

1 Eisenberg of "The Social Network"
2 Ladybug's prey
3 Gets a head?
4 "-phobia" start
5 Title woman in a Beach Boys hit
6 Meditation sounds
7 Back muscles, briefly
8 "___ Mio"
9 Went long
10 Painters Rivera and Velázquez
11 Expects
12 Children's author Asquith
13 1994 film based on an "S.N.L." skit
14 Provoke
15 Challenge for a playboy
16 "Carmen" composer
17 "Better safe than sorry," e.g.
18 Al Kaline, for his entire career
24 Best at an inspection, say
29 Pale
31 Do some farmwork
34 World leader in 1979 headlines
36 Record
37 What toasters often hold
38 Work night for Santa
40 Pulls back
41 It's found in cakes
42 Scrapes
44 Put up
45 Cig
48 Half of half-and-half
49 Run easily
50 Ran
52 Cheerleaders' practice
53 Generally
54 Original name of Motown Records
55 Hershiser who once pitched 59 consecutive scoreless innings
58 High-minded sort?
59 Old orchard spray
62 Is biased
63 City in Los Lobos?
65 Steers, as a ship
68 Osso buco need
69 Hindu deity
70 Idea
71 ___ John's
72 Part of FEMA: Abbr.
76 Woody offshoot?
77 News station
79 Like sports games and musical works
82 Bit of cosmetic surgery
84 Really bothered
85 Dutch treaty city
86 Cell component, for short
87 Have trouble with sass?
89 ___ moment
90 Marshy region
94 Source of the quote in 6-Across
95 Run out of gear?
96 Like nobles
98 "Finally!"
99 Hosting, informally
100 Some meditation teachers
101 Cousin of a camel
102 Nicked
103 Long-legged fisher
105 Martin's partner of old TV
106 Gasket variety
107 Bone: Prefix
110 Gym count
112 Workplace welfare org.
115 Never, in Neuss
117 Tick (off)

by Peter A. Collins

ACROSS

1 Polishes
8 Hearing at a hearing?
15 Deductive
16 A little reading at the supermarket checkout?
17 Literally, "military commanders"
18 Seconds
19 Book of ___
20 Grilled, on a menu
22 Grp. involved in much diplomacy
23 War of 1812 battle site
24 Huff
25 Ousts
27 Leave suddenly
29 "M*A*S*H" extra
31 Michaels of rock and reality TV
32 Act of God, e.g., in a contract
35 Stingers, of a sort
38 Really build up
39 Hip-hop's ___ tha Kyd
40 Provider of shock value?
43 Prefix with chemical
44 Animated film franchise starting in 2011
45 Gossipy affair
49 Talk ___
51 Figure also called the crux ansata
53 Something not to be believed
54 ___ story
55 ___ Jerry, band with the 1970 hit "In the Summertime"
57 "Into Thin Air" setting
58 Mother who had a bone to pick?
60 Faith that preaches nonviolence to all living beings
62 Not confined
63 Bedamn
64 "The only institution in the world which has been dying for four thousand years," per John Steinbeck
65 Doesn't stop

DOWN

1 Reveled (in)
2 Call from on high
3 Gambol
4 Cover of the Bible?
5 Under: Fr.
6 It might have decorative feet
7 Fibonacci, e.g.
8 Smaller than small
9 ___ Air
10 1983 Joel Schumacher film
11 Johann ___, opponent of Martin Luther
12 Istanbul is on it
13 Ten Commandments subject
14 Like Internet memes
21 Lure
24 Less stiff
26 It's an honour: Abbr.
28 Come out of one's shell, maybe
30 Like one side of the Aral Sea
33 Cilantro source
34 Come together
35 Service higher-up
36 Blabber
37 Focus of over 4,000 clubs around the world
41 Ad ___
42 Really bothered (by)
46 Jungle herbivores
47 Top-level
48 Team logo spot
50 The first one opened in Garden City, Mich., in 1962
52 Noted Greek officer
56 Itch
57 Terse compliment
59 Bellwether's call
61 Top gun

by Josh Knapp

6 CHANGELINGS

ACROSS

1 Hirer/firer
5 Iron setting
10 Food processor setting
14 One with accounts, for short
19 Darn, e.g.
20 Jets or chargers starter
21 Doozy
22 Revolutionary patriot Silas
23 Asian cuisine
24 Put in the minimum stake
25 Actress Lena
26 Willing to do
27 Gigantic sled hauls firewood quite a bit
31 1970s–'80s TV sheriff
32 Tell a story
33 Grub
34 Domestic worker claimed shifting beach engulfed basin
43 Hong Kong, e.g.: Abbr.
44 No-no on gym floors
45 Voting no
46 Band news
48 Put an end to
51 Catastrophic start or end?
52 Word after camper or before Camp's
53 Fused
54 It may go from sea to shining sea
55 Word in many California city names
56 Blue
59 "You wish!"
60 Friends who have never been to the beach don't walk by the girl so often
64 Characteristic times
65 Driver's assignment: Abbr.
66 Arrangement of hosing?
67 Children show their affection for model Kate above all others
76 Comics canine
77 Energetic sort
78 "That's ___-brainer"
79 Stuffing ingredient
81 "Waking ___ Devine" (1998 movie)
82 Hubbub
83 Solution for some housework
84 Villain
85 [I am shocked!]
87 ___ Romeo
89 Generic
91 Lines around Chicago
92 Boisterous oaf confused the previous set of actors
97 Outdoor party
98 Info for a limo driver
99 "Ta-ta"
100 Mr. Chamberlain intends to top off his gas tank
109 Capital where snail noodle soup is popular
110 Pew, for one
111 Coquette
112 Sly
113 When prompted
114 Sleeveless item, for short
115 Like some brewing containers
116 Mosque leader
117 Bog accumulations
118 Head of a Tatar group
119 Comics canine
120 Early 1900s gold rush locale

DOWN

1 This and that
2 Home of Hanauma Bay
3 Solo, in a way
4 BP logo shape until 2000
5 QB who led the Cowboys to victories in Super Bowls VI and XII
6 Varnish ingredient
7 Art Deco artist
8 First person to die in the Bible
9 Adjust, as pitch
10 Shut
11 Oceanic body
12 This and that
13 Strong and sharp
14 Majority group
15 Silt, e.g.
16 Whole bunch
17 Nephew of 8-Down
18 As stated in
28 "Was ist ___?"
29 Bombay and Boodles
30 H. H. Munro pseudonym
34 This and that: Abbr.
35 Music grp.
36 Actress Massey
37 Model add-on
38 Composer Camille Saint-___
39 Cars once advertised with the slogan "Find your own road"
40 Record of the year
41 "Necktie"
42 Mila of "That '70s Show"
47 Court V.I.P.'s
49 Literature's Nan or Gay
50 Supply room worker
52 Metaphors for serious headaches
55 Flip
56 "Midnight Cowboy" role
57 Loop around the West?
58 Mil. Decorations
59 "Sometimes you feel like a nut" nut
61 Not free
62 Super
63 Pago Pago locale
67 "King ___"
68 Toy company that made Betsy Wetsy
69 Playground comeback
70 Bungle
71 Upset with
72 Quaint contraction
73 "Love Story" costar
74 The Beach Boys' "Surfer Girl" vis-à-vis "Little Deuce Coupe"
75 Works
80 Egg holder
83 California city where the first Apple computer was built
84 "Hush!"
86 Retreat
87 "There oughta be ___"
88 Comedian who said "Every day starts, my eyes open and I reload the program of misery"
89 Cry of innocence
90 Non-PC person
93 Border payments
94 Kept
95 1960s chess champion Mikhail
96 Halloween prop
100 Die down
101 Early cultivator of potatoes
102 Mrs. Rabin of Israel
103 "Rama ___ Ding Dong" (1961 hit)
104 Show bias
105 Like some lashes and tans
106 Fendi ___ (men's cologne)
107 Activity at a doctor's office
108 Tick-borne affliction
109 Leapfrog

by Joe Krozel

ACROSS

1 "I swear . . ."
7 Dazzle
10 Trail near a hill?
14 Slanted coverage?
15 "Sounds like a plan!"
17 Hungarian liqueur sold in green bottles
18 Ancient Moorish palace in Granada
19 Like many motorcycle jackets
21 Vandal, e.g.
22 Entertains
23 Reached quickly, quickly?
25 Meaningful language unit
26 Early-morning risers?
28 Radar-using org.
29 Flamed out at a casino, say
33 Something done on a case-by-case basis?
34 "Sheesh! What's the world coming to?!"
35 Green on the screen
36 Voiced, in phonetics
37 Crunch producer
41 "Dang it!"
42 German-born photographer Barth
45 Requirement of Mormonism
47 Fragrant Clorox brand
49 Taking to the streets
51 Cushiony fabric
52 Education standards, e.g.
53 Food item whose name means, literally, "lightning"
54 Washington athlete
55 Scene
56 Like an atrium

DOWN

1 Red state?
2 Person who might ask "Did you hear . . . ?"
3 Given name of Augustus and Caligula
4 Like much music of the '90s
5 Sitcom stage, e.g.
6 What you can never win going away
7 Like
8 Make one
9 Daughter of Theodore Roosevelt
10 Blend
11 Popular Christmas trees
12 Something found on a dirt road
13 Ogle
16 First or second call, maybe
20 Gives
24 Ohio university nicknamed "Big Red"
26 Hugely
27 Card game also known as high-low-jack
29 Took down the garden path
30 They may put you to sleep
31 Graceful architectural curve
32 Folk singer __ Axton
33 Begin eagerly
34 Dialect of SE England
38 Certain sorority member
39 Like the Rolling Stones album "Get Yer Ya-Ya's Out!"
40 Gay partner?
42 Routine
43 Traditional Japantown feature
44 News __
46 Bag handle?
48 __ May Clampett of old TV
50 Brace

by Kevin G. Der

ACROSS

1 Hairstyle that usually involves clips or pins
8 Confidentially
15 N.J. Army base
20 "Beautiful!"
21 Points in the right direction
22 "Let's stop fighting, O.K.?"
23 "Those wreaths all look the same to me!"?
25 Something hard to drink?
26 Law school class
27 Start of a conclusion
28 Satisfies
30 Sales force, informally
31 Summers on the Seine
32 Convention closing?
33 ___ black
34 Cutlass model of the 1980s–'90s
36 Senile sort
39 Start of an oral listing of African nations, perhaps?
42 Texas home of the Bears
44 One small sip
46 Store
47 Asked to come back, in a way
49 "Over There" subj.
50 VCR button
51 D halved
52 Alternative to JFK
53 Showing less cleavage?
58 "Watch it!"
59 Many a critic's preference
61 Superbright
62 Mrs., abroad
64 Himalayan myth
65 Remote button
67 "Lemme ___!"
69 March org.?
73 Rally killers in baseball: Abbr.
76 "Warm"
78 "There was the time . . ."
81 Middle of summer?
84 Cheap roadside assistance?
87 "I don't need to hear that," informally
88 Skip town
89 Big ___
90 Stick in a rack
91 Mistakes
93 Setting for most of "Moby-Dick"
95 Kind of TV
98 Liqueur flavorers
99 Knockoff dress labeled "Armani," say?
101 Rob
103 Popular Hispanic newspaper name
104 Rider's handful
105 Son of, in foreign names
106 Have legs
109 E.R. "A.S.A.P."
110 Devote
112 Longtime Yankee nickname
113 Less loopy
114 Ban competition
116 Caution to an orphan girl not to leave her wildebeest behind?
119 Reeves of "John Wick"
120 Enter stealthily
121 "With Reagan" memoirist
122 Ready followers?
123 One in a tight spot?
124 Did some edgy writing?

DOWN

1 Get together
2 Embroidery loop
3 Group of actors who all have stage fright?
4 Emulated Diana Ross (1970) and Justin Timberlake (2002)
5 How long it takes mountains to form
6 Roxy Music cofounder
7 Attentive dog owner
8 French sister
9 They may be bookmarked
10 "The Family Circus" cartoonist Keane
11 Castigate
12 Away, in a way
13 Republican politico Michael
14 "___ happens . . ."
15 National Do Not Call Registry overseer, for short
16 Ancient galley
17 Western vacation spot
18 Winter carnival attraction
19 Gen ___
24 Silents star Bara
29 They put points on the board
33 Help to secure a loan, maybe
35 "Them's fightin' words!"
37 Former A.L. manager who was an N.L. M.V.P.
38 Geometric figures
39 Have a big mouth?
40 Attire
41 In a bad way
42 Secure, as a sailor's rope
43 She's asked "When will those clouds all disappear?" in a 1973 #1 hit.
45 Where many people may follow you
48 Per ___
54 Popular après-ski place
55 Spot in the afternoon?
56 Product that's hard to keep in stock
57 Janvier, across the Pyrenees
60 Cap
63 Supply with weaponry
66 Put away
68 Subway Series team
70 Lovely but stupid person?
71 U.S. city whose name becomes another city's name if you change both its vowels to A's
72 Kiss drummer Peter
74 Reach the Mediterranean, say?
75 Pig sounds
77 Fix, as some lawn chairs
79 Canine cousin
80 "Dallas" family name
81 Race in classic science fiction
82 "Whirlybird" source
83 Suspect duplicity
85 Caspian Sea feeder
86 Trojan horse, e.g.
92 Like the Parthenon
94 Fitting one inside the other
95 Appointment book
96 Did a 1930s dance
97 Big brother
100 Luxor Temple deity
102 Natural
105 Ryan of old TV
107 Intuit
108 Straight, now
109 Fifth Avenue retailer
111 Campaign grps.
112 Backwoods con?
113 Heavyweight bouts?
115 Indigo Girls, e.g.
117 Commercial lead-in to Pen
118 Lead-in to meter

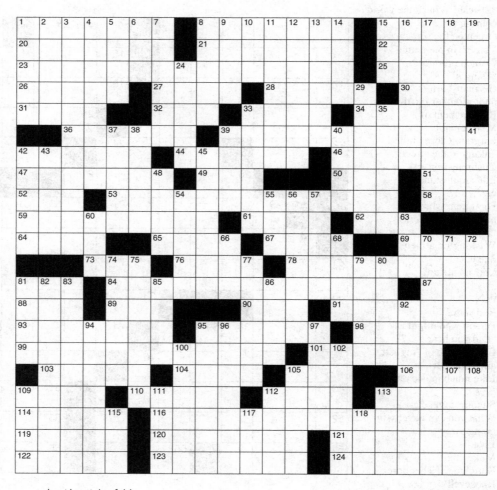

by Alan Arbesfeld

ACROSS

1 Thickburger seller
8 Some gathering spots
15 Iris features
16 Officially request
17 Alternative to a babka
18 Very abruptly
19 See 34-Down
20 "I can go for this!"
22 Beethoven's fifth?
23 As is fitting
25 Many old terminals
26 Shortening for shortcuts
27 It means everything to Erhard
29 Obituary word
30 It's often shifted after being laid
31 He began his third presidential term in 2014
33 Part of a goth dude's look
35 Party rule, for short
37 What holds up well?
38 "Puh-leeze, save the tears"
42 Cry before some clinking
45 Like Grieg, to Grieg
46 Common combo vaccine
48 It's not much higher than a D
50 Conjugation part between "sommes" and "sont"
51 Seeds often have them
52 Something developed casually?
53 See 54-Down
54 Himalayan food, maybe
57 In a lather, with "up"
58 "No sweat!"
60 "You don't have to tell me that"
62 Really opens up
63 You might take a cue from this
64 It's measured in points
65 Warriors in li'Illiade

DOWN

1 Its motto is "From sea to sea"
2 Plant called "rocket" outside the U.S.
3 Hands down, in a way
4 Footnote abbr.
5 Tear into
6 Copacetic
7 Land on the sea
8 "I'd like some of that, bro"
9 Cousins of harriers
10 Take __ off
11 Ketchup, e.g.
12 His servant is Kurwenal, in opera
13 "Try it . . . that's all I ask"
14 Person breaking his word?
21 "__ to disagree"
24 Minion's reply
26 Shear
28 Give it a go?
30 Fellow
32 "How could I do that?!"
34 19-Across units: Abbr.
36 General figure
38 80 chains or 8,000 links
39 It's in high demand
40 Chicken choices
41 Carlos the Jackal raided its HQ
43 Song with the lyric "Until we meet again"
44 Not quite yet
47 Logo displayer, maybe
49 Animistic figures
51 Turning phenolphthalein pink
54 With 53-Across, Italian sugar
55 Post-Passover period
56 __ siege (1993 newsmaker)
59 Special feeling?
61 Like some wit

by Tim Croce

ACROSS

1 Filling entrees?
9 Imperfect
15 Laugh track content
20 Former Diet Pepsi spokesmodel
21 Nymph jilted by Paris
22 "The Vampire Diaries" protagonist
23 Content of a demand to attend?
25 Cry of frustration
26 ___ flakes
27 Hullabaloo
28 Square meal?
30 Gas station adjunct
32 Freaky funeral noise?
37 Tornado Alley state: Abbr.
38 Smirnoff Ice, e.g.
40 Red-faced
41 View from Big Ben
43 Patriots' and Seahawks' org.
44 "Castaway" director, 1986
46 Points of view
48 W.W. II rationing agcy.
49 Dive from a fire-breathing creature?
53 Al Qaeda stronghold
55 Vegetable that's often fried
58 Place first, second or third, say
59 Man of letters?
61 "The Bridge on the River Kwai" director
63 Certain embedded Internet video
65 ___ lupus (gray wolf)
67 Not there yet
68 Company that introduced Saran Wrap
71 Venti, vingt or zwanzig?
75 Missal storage site
76 Coffee bean variety
78 Went on a run?
79 43-Across ball carriers: Abbr.
81 Lake ___, biggest lake in South America
84 Holdups
86 Perfumery measure
90 Workers' rights org.
91 Wool source
93 Woe for a sunburned sea monster?
95 Northern California's ___ River
97 Burn
99 Make hot
100 ___-Magnon
101 Uses mouthwash, e.g.
104 Like a dutiful sentry
107 Faux pas
109 Symbol on a sarcophagus
110 Intel products used at a nuclear facility?
113 Hit with a charge
114 Seiji Ozawa, e.g.
116 "Argo" setting
117 Roman guardian spirit
118 Diminish in strength
119 Overseeing a work crew, e.g.?
127 Cause of radioactivity
128 Beggar's receptacle
129 Attorney's presentation
130 Coeur d'___
131 Part of a contract
132 Mess

DOWN

1 Game show V.I.P.'s
2 Three-vowel word that sounds like a fourth vowel
3 Like some knights and warships
4 Kind of paste
5 What a spoiler might spoil
6 Golfer Woosnam
7 Chi-town circlers
8 Possessions
9 Old fogy
10 "We'd better skip it"
11 Santa ___ winds
12 Got the gold
13 Envelope abbr.
14 Handle of a plow?
15 Unceremonious removal
16 Half a game name that rhymes
17 Feathers, pointy bill, long legs, etc.?
18 "Life of Pi" director
19 Old colonial masters
24 Aficionado
29 AIDS-fighting drug
30 One with a colorful coat?
31 Woodard of "Primal Fear"
32 Garbage collector, informally?
33 Slanted columns
34 Fay of "King Kong"
35 Upped
36 Plant swelling
39 Like Isaac Asimov
42 Speed skater Ohno
45 Words of thanksgiving
47 Common craps roll
50 Dribble glass, e.g.
51 California resort town
52 Feelings of guilt
54 What I will always be, alphabetically
56 Parking lot figure
57 From square one
60 Problems with hoses
62 Skeletal enemy in Mario games
64 ___ point
66 Perform terribly
68 "Lookin' good!"
69 Kind of contraception
70 Period when rabbits stop fighting?
72 Harangues, with "at"
73 Sport
74 Mystery prize
77 Naïfs
80 Slangy greeting
82 Salad bar morsels
83 Like the world's largest sultanate
85 Economize to a fault
87 Juicy fruit
88 Destination of NASA's Dawn probe
89 What Othello and Desdemona do in "Othello"
92 Prime Cuts brand
94 Site of ancient Greek Olympics
96 What the jack of spades lacks
98 Howard Stern rival
101 Howard Johnson rival
102 Chilean author Allende
103 "My dear man"
105 Difficult situation
106 Greater or lesser follower
108 New York's ___ Island
111 Circular opening?
112 Gather (from)
115 "South Park" boy
117 Some PC screens
120 Many an art museum piece
121 Cellular messenger
122 Bit of old French bread
123 Charlottesville inst.
124 Picayune quibble
125 Brass producer, briefly
126 Catchy thing?

by David Steinberg

ACROSS

1 Ameche's "Moon Over Miami" co-star, 1941
7 Hit radio comedy about a bridge-playing couple
15 Decide, as a motion
16 Lacking inflection
17 Source of the quote "Change is certain"
18 Hurly-burly
19 Red cabbage juice, in chemistry class
21 Trail
22 Where "Desperately Seeking Susan" appears in the film of that name
23 Lee label, for short
24 The U.S. Open is played on it: Abbr.
25 Moniker after a lifestyle change
26 Cavaradossi's lover
27 Disco fabrics
28 Steels
29 Wasn't consistent
32 Providers of housewarmings?
33 Ace high?
34 Roy ___, title character in "The Natural"
35 Well-lit spaces
36 Super Bowl XX-winning coach
37 Title "Mr." in a Milne play
40 Some jewelry stores, informally
41 Queen who rallied the Dutch resistance in W.W. II
43 ___ card
44 Ball boy?
45 Attempt to spur demand
47 Rides
48 License to drill
49 Part of a suspended sentence?
50 Banquet offering
51 Like some rolls

DOWN

1 Producer of a cough and shivers
2 Decoratively pleated and gathered, as some bridal gowns
3 Soloist on the "Green Hornet" theme
4 Gatherings for hippies
5 Wimbledon is played in it
6 Some Navy specialists
7 Preserves, in the end
8 Arterial tree components
9 Hair holder
10 ___ Grace
11 N.C.A.A. division?: Abbr.
12 Come together
13 Beautifier
14 Reclaimed material used in jewelry
20 Cried harshly
23 Resolutions, e.g.
26 Madiba, for Nelson Mandela
27 ___ Stadium, home of the San Francisco 49ers
28 Former senator and presidential candidate who once dated Debra Winger
29 Foible
30 The planet in the sci-fi classic "Forbidden Planet"
31 Like American cheese
32 1980s P.M. nicknamed "The Old Crocodile"
34 Avery product for note-takers
36 What old things fall into
37 Holders of pieces of eight?
38 Humorously
39 Good for rushes, say
41 "___ Do It!" (Rosie the Riveter motto)
42 MX-5 maker
44 "It Ain't All About the Cookin'" memoirist
46 First noncanonical psalm in the Bible

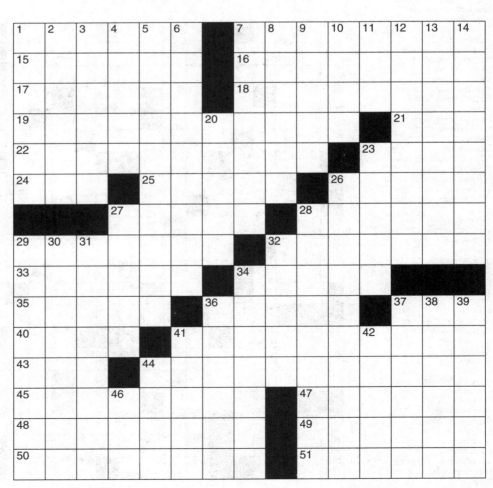

by Byron Walden

ACROSS

1 You may find it on your hands or side
5 Use a scalpel on
9 "O.G. Original Gangster" rapper
13 One connected with the force?
17 Not as brazen
19 It's worth $200 in Monopoly
21 Princess of Power from 1980s cartoons
22 Get noticed
24 Wiped
25 DuVernay who directed "Selma"
26 100%
27 Ring call, for short
28 More hot
30 "Sounds about right"
32 In stitches
34 Knocking
37 Load of money
38 Like some windows
40 Easily defeats, in sports
42 ___ Vogue
44 JFK probers
45 You may put stock in it
46 Director Coen
47 Enterprise for which a 14-year-old Buffalo Bill worked
51 One of 15 until 1991: Abbr.
52 "Baywatch" stars often jogged in it
54 Brownie unit
55 Japanese "yes"
57 ___ Nova (musical style)
60 Will, given the chance
62 Ninny
63 Dickens heroine
64 Cold-climate cryptid
66 End for an organisation's name
67 Exploit a loophole, say
71 Radio knob abbr.
72 Switch off
74 Unjammed
75 Cable airer of vintage films
76 Feeling low
78 Word between two last names
79 Trouble
80 Conductor announcements
82 Baloney
83 Newswoman Curry
85 Lean back and enjoy the ride?
88 Jumbo-sized
91 ___ fide
92 A Giants giant
93 Pick out
96 Washington landmark that lent its name to a Senate committee
98 Equally
101 Get the show on the road
103 Pursued, as perfection
104 Big bra feature
106 Sticks in a purse?
108 Rotten
110 Little ___
111 Company with two lameds in its name
112 Lifesaver's inits.
113 Facetious string?
115 Big fall from the sky?
119 Large shrimp
120 Wavering wail
121 Like crayons
122 One of the Ivies, informally
123 Organization with an Exalted Ruler
124 Aid in identifying a bird
125 Insignificant

DOWN

1 Hero in a John Irving best seller
2 "Eureka!"
3 Sainthood prerequisite
4 It was a dark period for Poe
5 Short supply
6 *Like puberty at age 16
7 Fatal ending?
8 *Biter in Niger
9 Following behind
10 Specialty of Industrial Light & Magic, for short
11 Alphas might clash over them
12 Buff
13 *One making the rounds at a party, perhaps
14 Having an unfavorable outlook
15 Blunder
16 Bit of hope
18 Bad recollection?
20 Tattooed
21 Alternatives to cheddars
23 Peanut
29 Topmost part of a face
31 Persevere
33 Drill sgts., e.g.
35 What buckets are made in, for short
36 Ob-___
39 It may be a high percent for the 1%
41 Football stat
43 Chinese restaurant assurance
45 Natl. Courtesy Month
48 Disapproving (of)
49 Swank
50 *First spacecraft to orbit a comet (2014)
51 What always comes in halves?
52 With 59-Down, permanent . . . or, literally, a feature of the answers to the seven starred clues
53 Cider server
56 Certain operatic voices
58 Energize
59 See 52-Down
60 Symbol of equality, briefly
61 Ahab's father
63 Randy types
65 Variety
68 Underwater trap
69 Flat-bottomed boat
70 Hank's wife on "Breaking Bad"
73 *Car dealership option
77 Event with a cantina, maybe
80 ___ treatment
81 *Chooses in the end
84 Zombie Strike SlingFire Blaster, for one
86 Linear, informally
87 Amazon activity
88 Hurtful comments?
89 "Ridiculous!"
90 Agent 007, e.g.
91 Really involved
94 Long-reaching weapon of yore
95 More delish
97 Bit of baby talk
98 What a general may lead
99 *Goals for underdogs
100 "I'm such a ___" (klutz's comment)
102 Givens on "Wheel of Fortune"
105 Weightlifter's exercise
107 Went off
109 Yawn-inducing
113 Android runner, often
114 Poet's "prior to"
116 Arctic flier
117 Olympics host after London
118 Spotlight hog

by Jeremy Newton

ACROSS

1 Language introduced in 1995
11 Factor in force
15 "This is a surprise!"
16 Torts course taker, typically
17 Brand that supports women?
18 Major menace
19 Intern
20 Old sitcom family name
22 Scratch
23 Height
25 Be a motormouth
26 Bismarck-to-Billings dir.
29 It names an annual Sexiest Woman Alive
31 "Ten Days in a Mad-House" muckraker
32 Hankered
34 Hankering
35 Trap locale
36 Counterpart of "to"
37 Talked bull?
38 2004 film featuring Paris
39 Gangsters' counterparts, informally
40 Overseas alternative?
41 Man on a mission, maybe
42 Michele of "Glee"
43 Mother of Richard I
45 Abbr. after "Rev." or before "dev."
46 Head doc?
47 Cab and others
48 Sparks in old films
50 Blunts, e.g.
52 Big name in scales
56 Like many works with "To" in their titles
57 What's a big hit with the school board?
60 It's to be expected
61 Treat with pudding and graham crackers
62 __ Style Awards
63 They have an infamous gap

DOWN

1 2010 New York Times best seller subtitled "Sounds Like a Rainbow"
2 Sounds accompanying light bulbs?
3 Big name in laptops
4 Knock for a loop
5 Emulated a cat burglar
6 Short, imaginative tales
7 Chockablock

8 Words before a major pronouncement
9 Rate word
10 Fooled (with)
11 Subject to dispute
12 Top-selling app of 2010
13 Where a techie hooks up
14 About to crash, apparently
21 Application suffix
23 Free light shows
24 Con victim
26 Parlor product made with an iron
27 Cary Grant or Betty Grable
28 2011 Flo Rida hit with the lyric "She ain't no rock star, but she got groupies"
30 Like Confucius, often
33 "Mamma Mia" quartet

35 Grp. with the slogan "Every child. One voice"
37 Fabric used in adhesive pads
41 Excuse
43 Go too far, e.g.
44 Like some pickups
49 Classic record label that rejected the Beatles with the comment "Groups with guitars are on the way out"
51 Height
52 Olivia who won a Razzie for "Bolero" and "Conan the Destroyer"
53 Mate
54 Blunt hit
55 Exposes, old-style
58 Handel's "__, Galatea e Polifemo"
59 "Toy Story" dinosaur

by David Steinberg

ACROSS

1 "Everyone who's anyone is attending!"
8 Shoot for the moon
13 Much-anthologized Frank R. Stockton short story
20 Herald, as a new year
21 Mitchell heroine
22 One calling it quits
23 Is a rat
24 Chimes, e.g.
25 Short thing for a diva
26 Big ___
27 Rarely
29 Long John Silver, for one
31 Not standard: Abbr.
32 Word with coffee or water
34 Bird that's also the name of an Irish river
35 Sped
36 Canon competitor
38 Cookies with a "Golden" variety
39 Slowing, in music: Abbr.
40 Audible pauses
41 Knot again
42 Miranda warning receiver, informally
43 Remote button with "+" and "-"
45 Govt. construction overseer
46 Founded, on city signs
47 Word before "I didn't know that!"
49 Heavy metal band?
51 Some fraternity men
54 Proverbial matter of perspective
59 John who played Harold in the "Harold & Kumar" films
60 Question asked in classic 1970s ads
66 Jeopardized
67 Ask
69 Greek goddess of vengeance
70 Like Lake Mead or Lake Powell
71 Strunk and White topic
72 They're of no concern to cougars
73 "M*A*S*H" role
75 Cry from a damsel in distress
77 Part of I.M.F.: Abbr.
79 Stickup line
83 Just
86 Laughed harshly
88 Overstress
89 Foe of Mr. Fantastic in the comics
91 Reception vessel
92 Some samples
94 Figure skater Midori
95 "Now it makes sense!"
97 Mop & ___
98 Frontier sheriff's badge
100 In the style of
102 Whistleblower's target?
104 "Bye for now," in textspeak
105 Rummage (through)
107 No longer hungry
109 D.C. club
110 Indian music
111 Langston Hughes poem
112 William ___, British general in the Revolutionary War
113 Assist, as an outlaw
114 Colored like ink in "Love's Labour's Lost"
115 Song by the Clash on Rolling Stone's "500 Greatest Songs of All Time" list
119 Material for many a ski lodge
120 Part of an Adirondack chair
121 ___ Conference
122 Command to Fido
123 Before
124 Tech grad: Abbr.
125 Gets fixed
126 Parisian possessive
127 "Maid in Manhattan" star, informally
128 Rx signers
129 General ___ chicken

DOWN

1 Dot on a transit map
2 -
3 Cartoonist who wrote the caption "Well, if I called the wrong number, why did you answer the phone?"
4 Titter sound
5 Backspaces, say
6 Incense
7 Eve who wrote "The Vagina Monologues"
8 Mounted
9 -
10 Test ___
11 Beginning of an attorney's ending
12 Like four of the eight planets
13 Subjects of apprenticeships
14 Superman, e.g.
15 -
16 Rough position?
17 Ones in the oil field?
18 Historic filer for bankruptcy in 2013
19 Was lovesick, say
28 Blather
30 ___ Exchange
33 Cut (off)
37 April second?
44 Center of activity
45 Physicist Ohm
47 Virgil, for Dante
48 Queen of mystery
50 Flightless bird
52 Org. with the motto "Not for self but for country"
53 Battle of the Alamo, e.g.
54 "For ___" (store sign around Father's Day)
55 California's Santa ___ River
56 I.C.U. worker
57 -
58 Most feeble
61 -
62 Map part
63 "Life ___ Highway"
64 One given the velvet rope treatment, for short
65 Sigmoid shape
67 Get in line
68 Kind of question
74 Kernel keepers
76 Prefix with -form
77 Crabby
78 Female with a beard
80 -
81 Stone who co-created "South Park"
82 Cousins of clarinets
84 Little houses on the prairie
85 Indie band whose name means, literally, "I have it"
86 Brace
87 Anaïs Nin and Franz Kafka, notably
89 Straight shooters?
90 Family members
93 Please, to a Puritan
96 Sommelier
99 Angles
100 Baseball family name
101 Pompom wielder's cries
103 Sulking
106 Things found in a pyramid
108 Sacred symbol
116 ___ Library (Austin, Tex., attraction)
117 Atl. Coast state
118 -

by Ellen Leuschner and Jeff Chen

15

ACROSS

1 It's usually taken on a bus
10 Pact signed by Nixon
15 Nancy Drew never left hers behind
16 Saw
17 Needing no prep, in a way
18 Bait
19 Org. in "Argo"
20 It depicts a winged woman holding an atom
21 Beyond that
22 Not mussed
24 Loads, for many: Abbr.
25 Constellation near Ursa Major
26 Art film?
30 Unleashes (on)
31 Who said "Power has to be insecure to be responsive"
34 Brute
35 Observe
36 Tip-offs
37 It may be thrown in the mix
38 Take off
39 Animated character who's five apples tall
41 "Truth in engineering" sloganeer
42 Where the waves come in?
43 Dairy case units: Abbr.
44 Was taken in
45 Stay a step ahead of
49 Secure
51 Place for a rivulet
54 Part of HUD: Abbr.
55 Diamond, e.g.
56 Triton, to Neptune
58 Reisz who directed "The French Lieutenant's Woman"
59 Crowd
60 "Make Someone Happy" composer
61 It connects two pages

DOWN

1 Slug
2 Allegorical painting from Picasso's Blue Period
3 Field standouts
4 Paul, for one: Abbr.
5 Exhibit plasticity
6 Be present in large quantity
7 Widen, as a gun barrel
8 Ark finder, familiarly
9 University course, for short
10 Delayed, in a way
11 Woodcutter, e.g.
12 Star's spot
13 Phrase often stamped in red
14 #1 hit on the soundtracks for "Grumpy Old Men" and "Beverly Hills Chihuahua"
21 Former Miss America who ran for the U.S. Senate in 1980
23 Early writing materials
24 "Fifty Shades of Grey" protagonist Anastasia
27 Fetter
28 Facility
29 Mature
30 Bee, e.g.
31 She wouldn't take an affront sitting down
32 "Since you asked . . ."
33 It gets attention when it runs
40 Prie-dieu feature
44 ___ Belt
46 Italian city near the Slovenian border
47 Users may enter it
48 1-Across, for one
50 Famous last word
51 New Year's Eve ball-drop commentator beginning in 2003
52 Crowning
53 Un crime de ___-humanité
56 Duke, e.g.: Abbr.
57 University course, for short

by Doug Peterson and Brad Wilber

ACROSS

1 Furnishes
8 Bit of body art, for short
11 "St. ___ Fire" (Brat Pack film)
16 Book reviewer?
19 Expel, as from a club
20 Historical chapter
21 Turnpike turnoffs [intimidate, in a way]
23 Narrator of "Amadeus" [go to bed]
24 Pet food brand [recover lost ground]
26 Compassionate [finally become]
28 City of Light creator at the 1893 World's Fair
29 Welles of "The Third Man"
30 Dunderhead
31 Attaches, in a way
32 Barbershop sound
36 Dealer's enemy
38 Ridicule
41 Country with the longest coastline
44 Comic strip dog
45 Skateboarder's safety item [salaam]
51 Goodbyes [abate]
52 Flagman?
53 Point at the ceiling? [misbehave]
55 She's not light-headed [amass]
57 Embarrassing putts to miss
59 Cosmic balance?
60 Lit group
61 Film library unit
63 Guy's partner
64 Storied voyager
65 What each group of circled words in this puzzle does
69 Dark looks
73 Get some Z's
74 Subtle emanation
75 Concert poster info
79 Comic actress Catherine
80 Four-legged orphans
83 Activity done in front of a mirror [clearly define]
85 Office trash [resign]
87 Start of many rapper names
89 Upset stomach [consume]
90 Loud and harsh [start crowding the crotch]
91 ___ Tree State (Maine)
92 Like March Madness teams
93 Contentment
95 Theater giant?
96 Establishes
97 Release tension, possibly
102 Big tank
104 What sarongs lack
108 Finnish outbuilding
109 Control of one's actions [fall in great quantities]
114 Granite dome in Georgia [moderate]
117 Converses à la Tracy and Hepburn [pay in advance]
119 Athens landmark [arise]
120 Retro music collection
121 Do without a radiator
122 Over there
123 Brought on
124 Stan of Marvel Comics
125 Lectures

DOWN

1 Super Bowl highlights, to some
2 House on campus
3 Precamping purchase
4 Luxury hotel chain
5 Barrel racing venue
6 Printmaker Albrecht
7 Mixes up
8 Appetizer with puréed olives
9 Fuego extinguisher
10 Balustrade location
11 Physicist Rutherford after whom rutherfordium is named
12 Radiation shield material
13 Hosts, for short
14 Muesli tidbit
15 Electoral map division
16 Setting for a castle
17 Painter Uccello
18 City on the Nile
22 They're all in the same boat
25 "___ Late" (Ricky Nelson hit)
27 Banquet V.I.P.'s
31 Wild guess
32 Strikers' replacements
33 "Taxi" character Elaine
34 Greenlandic speaker
35 Glazier's supply
37 Estrangement
39 Detach (from)
40 Misfortunes
42 Fitting
43 Team with a mascot named Orbit
46 Firth of "The King's Speech"
47 Mattress size
48 Mr. ___ (soft drink)
49 Gillette brand
50 Like a dull party
53 Go across
54 Actress Swinton
56 Hanes purchase, informally
58 Slack-jawed
62 Big leap forward
64 Courters
65 Woodsy picnic spot
66 Brace
67 Divided houses
68 #4 for the Bruins
69 Plants in a field
70 I.M.'ing session
71 Longship propellers
72 Summons, e.g.
75 Bamboozles
76 Brief digression
77 Fundamental principle
78 Quaint oath
80 Writer Richard Henry ___
81 Goes (for)
82 Nickname for a lanky cowboy
84 ___ Jemison, first African-American woman in space
86 Sport with double touches
88 To one way of thinking
91 Unseen danger
94 Nevertheless
97 English assignment
98 Knife brand
99 Iroquoian tribe
100 Before long
101 Boutonniere's place
103 Keyboard abbr.
105 Swinging occasion?
106 "West Side Story" heroine
107 Unfriendly dog sound
109 One of a bridge foursome
110 Smelly
111 Check mark
112 Book of Mormon prophet
113 Brisk pace
115 Brother of Shemp
116 Getting on
118 ___-pitch

by Patrick Berry

ACROSS

1 Summer suit accessory
10 Second installment
15 Classic symbol of rebellion
16 "Bluebeard's Castle," e.g.
17 Finishes freaking out
18 One of Utah's state symbols
19 It serves many clients, briefly
20 Versailles votes
21 Nincompoop
22 Throw out
24 Bean seen on-screen
26 One of many made by Hitchcock
27 Some orders at Chipotle
29 Famous New Year's Eve party?
31 Some sorcery
33 Speed ___
34 Group of crackers, for short?
35 Like many basements
37 Crib unit
39 State of old, briefly
42 Linking brainstem part
44 Make an impression on
48 Laugh-inducing pic
51 Carrier with the WorldPass frequent flier program
52 Dealer's quick query
53 "Bluebeard's Castle" librettist Balázs
55 Name meaning "born again"
56 Evidence of a big hit
57 Dandy
59 Port. title
60 Rearward, to a rear admiral
62 Battlefield transport
64 Occasion for goat tying
65 Yawn-inducing
66 Apply
67 Greasy spoon appliance

DOWN

1 Farm litter
2 GPS display
3 Mean
4 SAT fill-in: Abbr.
5 Last name on a 40-Down
6 City that rivaled ancient Sparta
7 Like some owls
8 "Once more . . ."
9 Equivalent of several dashes: Abbr.
10 Kitty
11 Without feet
12 One who assumes control by default?
13 Stock handlers
14 "Stovepipe" of W.W. II
23 Sang
25 Most-watched show of 2012–13
26 Woodworker's tool
28 Apply haphazardly
30 Do-re-mi
32 One who's beyond picky
36 Opening piece
38 Way up
39 Some cookies
40 Holder of many a diorama
41 Musical embellishment
43 Where to get the lead out?
45 Not part of a series
46 Tourist destination on the Riviera
47 Mudslinger
49 Bit of headwear, in British lingo
50 Kind of disc
54 Cutlass successor
58 Water, e.g.: Abbr.
61 Squirt
62 Dating site initialism
63 Grp. whose seal featured Washington on horseback

by Barry C. Silk

ACROSS

1 "u r KIDDING!"
4 Doesn't tread lightly
10 Neighbor of a delt
13 1958 space monkey
17 Site of cataracts
19 Chillax
20 Goof
21 "Conversely . . . ," online
22 Pass
24 Setting of 118-Across
27 Language from which "tattoo" comes
29 Mens ___ (legal term)
30 Required
31 Star of 118-Across
35 "Roll Over Beethoven" group, briefly
36 Chemistry lab droppers
37 Luggage checker, for short
38 Hearing something?
43 Author LeShan
44 Botanist Carl Linnaeus, for one
48 With 65-Down, 160-year-old fraternity founded at Miami University of Ohio
49 Opening lyric of 118-Across
57 Complaints
58 Georgetown athlete
59 Send
60 Important factor in a crossword tournament
62 Eclipses, to some
64 Raid target
67 ___ Fridays
68 Duo behind 118-Across
77 Fútbol announcer's shout
78 See 130-Across
79 Lightly hammered?
80 "Cosi Fan Tutte," e.g.
86 "The Best Exotic Marigold Hotel" actress
89 Do some roof work
90 Port authority?
91 Honor for 118-Across
95 Sports bar fixture
97 Narnia girl
98 Curmudgeon's review
99 Fish dish
101 Prefix with city or centennial
103 Digressions
106 It ends in Nov.
108 Family upon whom 118-Across is based
111 Wynken, Blynken and Nod, e.g.
115 Whup
116 Recondite
118 Movie that opened on 3/2/1965
122 Superdietary, informally
123 "Pics ___ didn't happen" (slangy challenge)
124 "Wailing" instrument
125 Big export of Myanmar
126 Nine-month pregnancy
127 "Let's Make a Deal" features
128 Figure in a Sunni/Shia dispute
129 Where the Potemkin Steps are
130 With 78-Across, "Righto!"

DOWN

1 Two out of 11?
2 Nicki with the 2014 hit "Anaconda"
3 Dress to the nines
4 Rite Aid rival
5 Picks up
6 Checked out
7 "The culminating point that beauty has attained in the sphere of music," per Tchaikovsky
8 ___ crawl

9 Guy's name that's an alphabet run
10 Viola parts
11 Remove any trace of
12 1961 Disney villainess
13 Crime boss John
14 Not esta or esa
15 Disturb
16 2022 World Cup city
18 Food poisoning cause
23 Asian capital nicknamed the City of Azaleas
25 Hi-___
26 Does a real number on, say
28 Something a trypanophobe fears
32 In the slightest
33 Latin 101 verb
34 Trumpet sound
39 Go (through)
40 Citrus fruit
41 Official in a turban
42 Bit of filming
45 ___ de México (Mexico City daily)
46 A.L. East, e.g.: Abbr.
47 Paperless party planner's option
49 2011 Marvel film
50 ___ neanderthalensis
51 Checked out
52 "___ tight"
53 Singer Bareilles with the 2007 hit "Love Song"

54 Heaps
55 Interprets
56 Many a Silicon Valley worker: Abbr.
61 Heart
63 Maker of Dreamcast games
65 See 48-Across
66 Cave opening?
69 Eldest Stark child on "Game of Thrones"
70 Pivots
71 Rendezvous
72 File ___
73 Little songbirds
74 Bigger than big
75 Luzón, por ejemplo
76 Manhattanite, e.g., for short
80 Hooters
81 12 points
82 Cuts off
83 Senator William who pioneered a type of I.R.A.
84 Seminoles' sch.
85 Part of the food pyramid
87 Sicilian border?
88 Flight from danger
92 Orbit, e.g.
93 About
94 "Rats!"
96 Smartphone capability
100 Crown since 1952

102 Hookup in bed?
103 Annual awards in animation
104 Site of Spaceship Earth
105 Kevin of "House of Cards"
107 Unlike much Schoenberg music
108 Formula One driver ___ Fabi
109 Haven
110 Pitfall
111 "Comin' ___ the Rye"
112 Prince, e.g.
113 Lies
114 Year that Cambridge's St. John's College was founded
117 Stately trees
118 Kind of list
119 To's partner
120 Joe
121 Civil War inits.

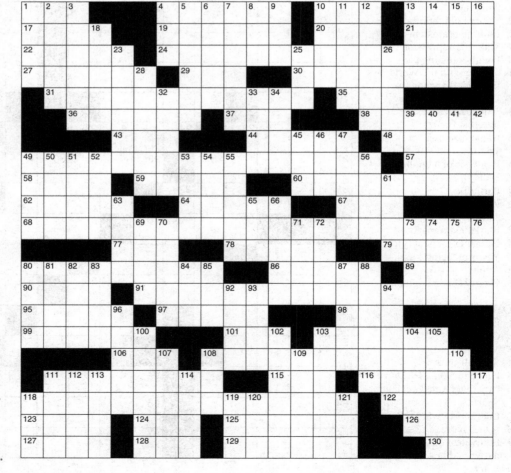

by Finn Vigeland

ACROSS

1 Completely
9 Southern river to Winyah Bay
15 Something you might make a stand for
16 Speaking part
17 Quaint raid targets
18 Minnesota county whose seat is Grand Rapids
19 A lot of bucks . . . or the Bucks, briefly
20 Tees off
22 Herbert of Hollywood
23 Hit 90, e.g.
25 Their pH's are often measured
26 Force user
27 Elusive giants
29 C. J.'s boss on "The West Wing"
30 Sickening thing
31 Boiling evidence
33 "See the difference a little drop can make" sloganeer
34 A in typing class, e.g.
37 Hodgepodges
38 "Hold your horses!"
39 Beaucoup
40 Modern back-and-forth
41 Model material
42 Unlikely to stress out
46 Makes one's bed?
47 Key of Debussy's "Claire de Lune"
49 What often produces passing thoughts?
50 Where the Saguenay R. flows
51 Boston area known for its brownstones
53 Execute a motion on the fly?
54 Still in development?
56 Pink application to red areas
58 Breezed through something
59 Debated, debated, debated
60 Place less value on
61 They use every letter 1-Across

DOWN

1 Very weak
2 It might tell you to chill
3 Cheese __
4 Descend upon in droves
5 Like Mr. X, briefly
6 Burdens
7 European Union anthem
8 Spiced up, say
9 Carries on steadily
10 Works on a course
11 Follower of Johnson or Kennedy
12 Source of a character flaw?
13 Some intelligence work
14 Checks
21 One of several awarded to Pres. Clinton
24 Strips of land, say
26 Sequel to Alcott's "Little Women" and "Little Men"
28 "Land __!" (quaint cry)
30 Like the best of friends
32 __ deck (gym machine)
33 Little sucker?
34 Group of dispatchers
35 Two tablespoons
36 "Science as a Vocation" sociologist
37 It's sometimes called a yellow turnip
39 Toadstool that exudes latex when cut
41 Sister of Pizza Hut
43 Cup-shaped forest fungus
44 Shady Records co-founder
45 Birds, e.g.
47 Writer about a hellish journey
48 Hook on a kite
51 Musical lead-in to pop
52 Light principle
55 Concubine's chamber
57 Follower of Salyut 7

by David C. Duncan Dekker

ACROSS

1 Exploit, e.g.
4 Mountain cat
8 All-___
11 Careen
15 "New Adventures in Hi-Fi" band
18 Thickness
19 Subject of a prophecy in Genesis
20 Ad ___
21 Eponymous Indian tribe
22 Cry on the bridge
23 The last one in, perhaps
25 Toledo-to-Akron dir.
26 "Why is a raven like a writing desk?" asker
28 Move quickly, as clouds
29 Shames into action
32 Puts on
33 Darlings
34 Cross
35 Confuse
37 Capital near the 60th parallel
38 Sushi coating, maybe
40 Currency in Turkey
41 Bully on "The Simpsons"
43 "___ no doubt"
45 Mess
46 2009 Newbery-winning author Gaiman
49 Where you might exchange tender for tenders
52 Something off the top of your head?
54 Particularly: Abbr.
55 Make content
56 El Amazonas, e.g.
57 Hole punchers
58 Heart-to-heart, e.g.
62 Shaving ___
63 Wood in Lucius Malfoy's wand
64 Chum
65 Setting for part of "Frankenstein"
69 With 94- and 72-Across, a mnemonic for the first eight digits of [symbol in the middle of the grid]
71 XV years before the Battle of Hastings
72 See 69-Across
74 "I" strain?
75 Jeremy of the N.B.A.
76 Like much of Italy in 700 B.C.
77 Encrusted
78 Atop
81 ___ Bay, site of a historic Admiral Perry visit of 1853
82 Israeli diet
85 Disquietude
86 "Carry on"
88 It never starts with 666: Abbr.
89 Beast imagined in "Beasts of the Southern Wild"
91 "That makes sense now"
93 Practice runners: Abbr.
94 See 69-Across
101 Trips up?
103 Computing pioneer Lovelace
104 Agitates
107 It's revolting
108 One way of learning, it's said
111 Parish head
113 Belch
114 Risky venture
116 Cropped up
117 Snitch
118 Fabled 90-Down
119 Needle case
120 Like two lowercase letters of the alphabet
121 Mormon V.I.P.
122 English author Blyton
123 1/2, for one
124 Brings around

DOWN

1 Bank inits.
2 Not far apart
3 As is usual
4 Remains unsettled
5 Exploit
6 Smith of "Downton Abbey"
7 Portends
8 Heat, informally
9 Breather
10 Stock of certain companies?
11 -
12 Like the previous clue (which originally read "Place of Jewish worship")
13 Red Cross work
14 Place to get clean
15 How questions may be asked
16 Derelict buildings, e.g.
17 Eau holder
24 Money in la banque or la banca
27 "Rolling in the Deep" singer
30 Bank inits.
31 "Where would ___ without you?"
33 Puts on
36 [Good heavens!]
38 Enter through the back door, say
39 Frat Pack member Ben
42 Slip-___
44 Slugger's stat, for short
47 "Who goes there?" response
48 Deadly
49 One end of the hotline
50 Pie part (that's appropriately placed in this puzzle?)
51 Arrivals
52 Betide
53 Be in store for
58 Threatens, as a king
59 "___ Heroes"
60 Like a body no longer at rest?
61 ×
65 N.A.A.C.P. or N.C.A.A. part: Abbr.
66 Trounced
67 Ladies' man
68 Church assemblies
70 Tobacco chewers' chews
73 With 79-Down, place to get spare parts
79 See 73-Down
80 Ear-related
83 Key material
84 Ballyhoo
86 Hide
87 Put on again
90 Race loser
92 Solve
94 It always points down
95 Football hiker
96 Bivouacked
97 Brouhahas
98 Struck (out at)
99 Escalator parts
100 What money can be kept in
101 Ear-related
102 Cry exclaimed while facepalming
105 More work
106 Actress Parker
107 Parcel (out)
109 Rani's wear
110 Bit
112 Chianti and Beaujolais
114 What's that in Italy?
115 Train track support

by Tom McCoy

ACROSS

1 Tie one on at dinner
11 Online heads-up
15 1990s TV cartoon produced by Steven Spielberg
16 Home for the College of Wooster
17 "Cash is king"
18 Role for Ferrell on "S.N.L."
19 Dear
20 "The __ Bridge Disaster" (McGonagall poem)
21 Runners' spot
22 Diamond __ Trucks (bygone company)
23 It's found on the toe of a boot
25 Goes for the gold?
27 Yogi's title
28 Bolivian export
30 Stick in the mouth?
31 Subject of a Hoyle treatise
33 Portrayer of Hector in "Troy"
35 Infomercial product said to hold 12 times its weight in liquid
37 Band with a 2000 Grammy-winning hit that's on Rolling Stone's list of all-time "most annoying songs"
38 Ones pulling strings?
40 Old-hat
41 Text-interpreting technology used with PDFs
42 Duke
43 Halfway house?
44 Hurdles
46 Step
48 Boston landmark, with "the"
51 George Knightley's love interest, in literature
52 Fired (up)
53 Some messages from messengers
55 Truncates
56 Mobbed by mosquitos
58 Not class-specific
59 1999 Crowe/Pacino film nominated for seven Oscars
60 Newspaper post
61 Things happy people do

DOWN

1 Hip-hop's Kendrick __
2 Quick snap time, in football
3 "Ding ding ding!"
4 Mr. of "Peter Pan"
5 Singer/songwriter whose name anagrams to ART OF SLY WIT
6 Med. specialist
7 Gaucho gear
8 Journalistic ideal
9 Like glop
10 Some undergrad degs.
11 Language from which "litmus" comes
12 Certain subterfuge
13 Well-calibrated
14 Savior of Little Red Riding Hood
24 Division of biology
25 Kind of nerve
26 Put through cycles, in a way
27 Boob
29 Mars or Neptune
31 Metaphor for a tedious, futile effort
32 Expresses grumpily
34 Pottery __
35 Wolfed (down)
36 Newborn stats: Abbr.
39 Figure in many New Yorker cartoons
45 Kind of surgery
47 Bit the dust
48 What the rainbow flag signifies
49 Go wild
50 Web browsers
52 "That's a funny one"
54 First name in the International Tennis Hall of Fame
56 "And stuff"
57 Fort Myers-to-Tampa dir.

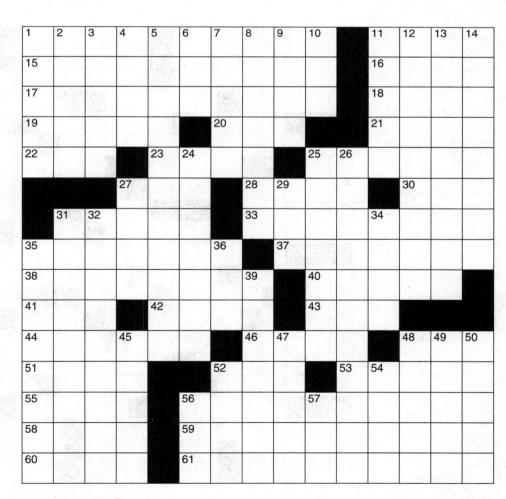

by James Mulhern

ACROSS

1 Opportunity
9 So-called Baghdad by the Bay
15 "___ at the office"
20 Mayor's title
21 Mr. Darcy's creator
22 Circle
23 "You can never moor a boat here"?
24 Provide sufficient coverage from risk?
26 Fashion portmanteau
27 Gets close to
29 "Have some!"
30 Feature of Hawaii's Molokini Crater
32 Some miracle drug pushers
35 Bothers
39 Atheistic Cuban leader?
43 Like Columbus
44 Low
45 Legendary weeper
46 Desk chairs?
48 Most common key of Chopin's piano pieces
51 Tour grp.
52 Side in the Peloponnesian War
53 Hit hard
54 Unsalvageable
56 Valentine and others: Abbr.
57 Pvt. Pyle's outfit
59 Get on
60 Quechuan "hello"?
64 ___-Caps
65 Moved a shell
67 Removing a Band-Aid too early?
70 2:1, e.g., in the Bible
73 On
74 Covering first, second and third base?
78 "Hello, Hadrian!"
79 Tear down, in Tottenham
81 A year in Brazil
82 Aristocratic
83 Certain tide
85 Green deli stock
87 With 115-Down, 1983 Lionel Richie hit
90 Subjects of some modern school bans
91 Add to the Video Clip Hall of Fame?
93 Is forbidden to, quaintly
95 Genre for Panic! at the Disco
96 Drink that might cause brain freeze
97 Diet?
101 Jack-in-the-box part
102 "Lucy" star, in tabloids
103 Bygone Chevrolet
104 Madonna's "Into the Groove," originally
106 "Do ___!"
108 Cameron who directed "Jerry Maguire"
112 Diapers?
117 Popular website whose name is a hint to this puzzle's theme
119 Shakespeare's "The Comedy of Errors," e.g.
120 How to make money "the old-fashioned way"
121 Disrespectful, in a way
122 ___ Mountains
123 Heavy-lidded
124 Visitor to a fertility clinic

DOWN

1 Sorority letters
2 Place for curlers
3 Home for King Harald
4 Shepherd formerly of "The View"
5 Stinko
6 Big picture: Abbr.
7 50–50 chance
8 It can be sappy
9 Parodist's principle
10 Charges
11 There's one every year for Person of the Year: Abbr.
12 Political analyst Rothenberg
13 Roll by a cashier
14 Long, unbroken take, in film lingo
15 Certain ancient Greeks
16 Small caves
17 ___ Dhabi
18 Bookie's charge
19 Ordinal ending
25 Something you might get two 20s for?
28 Mideast's Gulf of ___
31 Morn's counterpart
33 Bloods' rivals
34 Coastal region of Hawaii
36 What the Spanish Armada fought
37 Shakespeare's world?
38 Proven
39 Japanese porcelain
40 A drag
41 ___ acid (vitamin B9)
42 Interlocking piece
43 Became peeved
47 Oil-rich land ruled by a sultan
49 Writer Nin
50 Pair of fins
52 Bits of music
55 Atty. gen.'s employer
56 Word with get or smart
58 Some ski resort rentals
61 Throb
62 City about 100 miles ENE of Cleveland, O.
63 Paper featured in the documentary "Page One," for short
64 No. often between 15 and 50
66 Belligerent, in Britspeak
68 Three on a 6
69 Poorly
70 Go poof
71 Without variation
72 Get educated (on)
75 More outré
76 Memorable mission
77 Disinfecting Wipes brand
80 Like light that causes chemical change
81 "Gladiator" locale
84 Resistance
86 "Gladiator," for one
87 Smirnoff of comedy
88 "___ Como Va" (Santana hit)
89 Cold
92 Country singer Kenny
93 Grandeur
94 "Mazel ___!"
98 Bottom sirloin cut of beef
99 Made out
100 One who takes the bull by the horns
102 Plant part
105 Turns a different shade, say
107 Alternatively
109 Sleipnir's master, in myth
110 Drunk's favorite radio station?
111 App creator, perhaps: Abbr.
112 Uncertainties
113 '60s war zone
114 Back the other way
115 See 87-Across
116 Uptown dir. In N.Y.C.
118 –: Abbr.

by Dan Feyer

ACROSS

1 1968 hit with the line "I was raised by a toothless, bearded hag"
16 Theodore Dreiser travelogue
17 "Don't worry"
18 Sounds of confusion
19 Sounds of shock?
20 Has a part of?
21 What a buzzkill kills
22 Means of maritime defense
23 Virginia willow's genus
26 Sch. near Gulfport
28 Conjurer, old-style
32 Alternatives to lemon ices
37 Went from being picked on to picking on, say
38 Announcement start
39 Like racehorses
40 Classic Ford
41 Passing side?
42 Bon __
44 Kind of provider, for short
46 Words said before qualifying?
50 Cabinet dept.
52 __ Poke
55 Seriatim
58 Makes early progress
59 Question on public transportation

27 [wolf whistle]
28 Ally in a partnership
29 Take the edge off
30 V composition, perhaps
31 Indicators of possessiveness
33 45-Down, for one: Abbr.
34 It's observed as far west as Ind. in the summer
35 500 letters
36 Proverb follower?
42 Off-duty wear
43 Stephen King's "Uncle __ Truck"
44 "Spider-Man" actress
45 Hero of the Mexican-American War
46 Meditative sort
47 Chemical endings
48 Granite paving block
49 More than dis
50 Lakeside tribe
51 Olympic swimmer Torres

52 Common English lit subj.
53 Start of treason?
54 Opera conductor Daniel
56 Bad marks
57 Alternative to "?" in some listings

DOWN

1 Dick's running mate
2 Slip accompanier
3 Some slip-ons
4 Bluegrass genus
5 Trooper, e.g.
6 It comes before Iyar
7 "Go anywhere, do anything" sloganeer
8 Lab sounds?
9 Actor John of "American Pie" films
10 A hafiz knows it by heart
11 P.R. person
12 Swinging rhythm
13 Some prosecutors, for short
14 Wear over a petticoat
15 Service lines?
21 Spread out . . . or struck out
22 Hang over one's head
23 Drops in the bucket
24 What a saw often has
25 Give __ (mind)
26 Raise, in a way

by Frederick J. Healy

ACROSS

1 Seat at a hoedown
6 Brouhaha
10 ___ it up
13 Cliff Huxtable or Ward Cleaver
18 Like some muscles and baby food
19 Parks staying put
20 One for war?
21 Like the veal in osso buco
22 They can knock out lightweights
24 Sleep (with)
26 Pope during the rule of Emperor Constantine IV
27 Ghetto blaster?
28 Virgil epic
29 Slapped on, as paint
30 Jazz band instrument
31 Quality that's a bit unsettling
34 Whitesmith's medium
35 Watched some online videos
36 Like sweat and some moccasins
38 With 91-Across, super-antsy . . . or like 24 Across answers in this puzzle?
40 Mole hunter
41 Retired runway model
42 "Right you ___!"
44 Open to debate
45 2007 film featuring Raphael, Leonardo, Donatello and Michelangelo
46 Country singer Tucker
49 Slow
50 Final Four org.
52 "I must remember this for later . . ."
55 Ring
57 Dinner that was prepared hours ago, say
61 Opposite of totally
63 Drill (into)
64 Prove useful
65 Nice thing about purchases in Delaware and Oregon
66 Plays a ukulele
67 Moose or mouse
69 One getting hammered
70 Part of two state names
72 Authority over sheriffs in England
73 Down Under marsupial
75 Grp. that meets in Albany
77 Perv, e.g.
78 It's not so bad
79 Flimsy
80 Secretly adds to emails
81 "Tearin' Up My Heart" group
83 Feats of Keats
85 Sitcom alien
86 Something e-cigarettes lack
87 Seem
90 Coffee container
91 See 38-Across
94 Two notes from a tuba
97 Cupful before sleep, maybe
98 Bungler
99 Popular dessert in Georgia
101 It's at one end of a rainbow
103 Model add-ons
104 Spiff up
106 Boston skyscraper, with "the"
107 Driver's license, but not a credit card, e.g.
109 Chart for weighing options
111 Food processor?
113 Strips bare
114 Madeira Mrs.
115 "You must ___" (order to an earthling)
116 Brave
117 Stopping point
118 Water source
119 Richard of "Shall We Dance?"
120 Old-fashioned fraternity activity

DOWN

1 Targets of some cryosurgery
2 Facilities overseen by the C.D.C.
3 Adds
4 Playroom block
5 Swirled
6 Turkey Day follower: Abbr.
7 Hi-fi sound?
8 With suspicion
9 Lavender or lilac
10 Lights up
11 Flu symptom
12 Wasn't joking
13 Tromped (on)
14 Morrison who sang "Brown Eyed Girl"
15 Subside
16 ___ rifle
17 It's a first
21 Entity
23 Rag on
25 Pull (in)
32 Aussie "Mornin'!"
33 Nina who sang "I Put a Spell on You"
35 Kind of joke
37 When brunch might be served
39 "Whew!"
43 Pure bliss
45 Pinch
47 "It's sad but true . . ."
48 Eagles or Ravens
49 Capitol insiders
50 Bellini opera
51 Without a hitch
52 "Grand" mountain
53 Source of eggs
54 Some risqué communiqués
56 Many pages are written in it
57 Campus dining area
58 Captain America portrayer Chris
59 "Duck Dynasty" network
60 Source of bile
62 Steamed
63 Luxuriate
67 Apple Store display
68 There might be one on a car
71 Capital that's the seat of Lewis and Clark County
73 Amuse
74 Music-licensing grp.
76 "God's Son" rapper
77 Lot of junk
80 Show of respect
82 Cutting class?
83 Sketch
84 Get all decked out
85 Selfish, as an attitude
86 Credit (to)
88 Travel as a group, in a way
89 Liberals
91 Saturday morning fare, informally
92 "That's close enough!"
93 Peke or Pom
95 Many Manets
96 Get together
97 Encountered
100 More epic
102 Book before bedtime, maybe
104 One seeking money for a meter?
105 Vial liquids
108 Martin's wife on the 1990s sitcom "Martin"
110 "What'll ___?"
112 Closely monitor

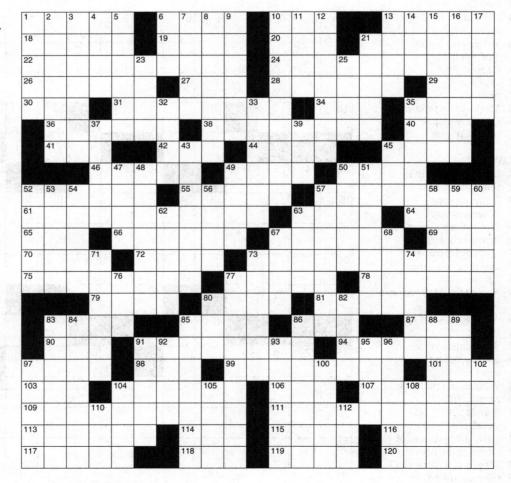

by Jeremy Newton

ACROSS

1 Hair-raising experience for a beachgoer?
10 Cry of mock enthusiasm
15 Bypass brand names, say
16 Hyperrealist sculptor Hanson
17 Planet pulverizer of sci-fi
18 "Today" co-anchor Hill
19 Composer of the opera "Fiesque"
20 What an au pair might study, briefly
21 One of a set set in hair
22 Bygone military commander
23 Increase the pitch of
25 He worked with the illustrator Phiz
26 Tough to resolve
28 Catch but good
29 Computer command
30 Western shocker
32 "Jeweler of kings, king of jewelers," per Edward VII
34 Harum-___
37 Setting for un'opera
38 It has rules for writers
40 Stand
41 Natural pain reliever
42 Chain for a mechanic
44 Like new bills
48 Fluffy toy, familiarly
49 Novel opinions, informally?
51 It fell after 15 years
52 "Jeepers!"
54 32-Across offering
55 Word of caution
56 Like some broken pledges?
57 They're taken to go
59 Expert
60 Periodical whose first shared cover featured Michelle Obama
61 Six-pack container?
62 Option for giving food a bite

DOWN

1 Rowdydow
2 Big chill?
3 Some joeys
4 ___ pieces
5 Overseas drama
6 Response to "Need anything else?"
7 Point of exasperation
8 Spring-blooming bush
9 Kid who had an original Rubik's Cube, e.g.
10 Classical music venue
11 Cast
12 Under-age temptation
13 Quick examination
14 Beginning of time
21 Apply
23 Some cough medicine
24 34-Down item
27 Major indulgence
29 Best successor
31 Musandam Peninsula populace
33 Change color, maybe
34 Disappearing communication system?
35 Home of the Canyon of the Ancients
36 Perfume delivery option
39 Colloquial pronoun
40 Need to practice?
43 Microsoft's Age of Empires, e.g.
45 Apple app for video editing
46 Emergency alerts
47 Like many radio stations
49 Prompted
50 Late stage, of sorts
53 Fires (up)
55 Opposite of flatness
57 Modern lead-in to cat
58 Lick

by David Steinberg

CALIFORNIA, HERE I COME

ACROSS

1 Small drums
7 Leaves of grass
13 Folded like a fan
20 East Coast national park
21 Early stone tool
22 Go wild
23 Ancient Peruvian using Netflix?
25 Washington post?
26 Newbie: Var.
27 Senator Mike from Wyoming
28 1965 hitmakers Dino, ___ & Billy
30 Start to lose it
31 Exactly 72, maybe
33 "No fishing here!"?
38 Be up
39 Ending with Vietnam
40 Vietnam ___
41 Like the headline "ELVIS FATHERED MY ALIEN BABY"
42 Sheer
44 Lines from Homer and Erasmus
47 Some art projections
51 Dog whose rocket went off course?
55 Make the podium
56 Some black-tie events
57 Refrain syllable
58 "Network," for one
59 Never
62 "Is that so?"
64 A minimus is a little one
65 Comment to an annoying blackjack dealer?
71 TV ET
72 Pub fixture
73 "Ta-da!"
74 Up-to-the-minute
77 Letters after Sen. Kirsten Gillibrand's name
78 Less deserving of a laugh, say
81 Sealer, maybe
82 Part of a jumbo trail mix?
87 Sorry sort
89 Lit
90 Marie Antoinette, par exemple
91 First name on the "America's Got Talent" panel
93 State on the Miss.
94 Bouncer's concern
96 AAA offering: Abbr.
97 Agent for Bogart's partner?
102 Wild
104 Declare
105 Filmmaker Riefenstahl
106 Hold it!
108 "When I was ___ . . ."
109 President John Tyler's wife
111 "12-Point Type: A History"?
116 Tied up
117 They might grab some food before a flight
118 Hard and unyielding
119 Bar order that's not drunk
120 "Me as well!"
121 Isn't completely truthful

DOWN

1 It may be on the tip of your tongue
2 Put in play
3 It holds a lock in place
4 Classic theater
5 Marshy place, perhaps
6 Identical to
7 Auto pioneer Karl
8 "When dealing with people, let us remember we are not dealing with creatures of ___": Dale Carnegie
9 Will Smith biopic
10 When repeated, a child's meal
11 Yadda, yadda, yadda
12 Tangerine or peach
13 Force divided by area, in physics
14 ___ brothers, inventors of the motion picture (1895)
15 Having five sharps
16 Cause of a great loss?
17 Option for a quick exit
18 Quaint letter opener
19 Classic British Jaguar
24 Concerning
29 Sharp turn
32 Projected image
34 High-tech surveillance acronym
35 Major account
36 Site of a 1776 George Washington victory in the Revolutionary War
37 ___ Rudolph, U.S. sprinter who won three golds in the 1960 Olympics
43 British racetrack site
44 ___ Hardware
45 It's in the 60s
46 Rock singer?
48 Photoshop user, e.g.
49 Egyptian king overthrown in a 1952 revolution
50 Wintry mixes
52 Barely touch, as a meal
53 Visibly stunned
54 Grp. with a launch party?
58 Criticism
59 Spiral-horned antelopes
60 "C'est magnifique!"
61 Like some titmice
62 Fist bump, in slang
63 It might say "Happy Birthday!"
66 Ancient Assyrian foe
67 Old lab burners
68 Ambushed
69 One calling foul?
70 Mess (around)
75 Catholic rite
76 "Delphine" author Madame de ___
78 Waxing and waning, e.g.
79 U.K. honour
80 Free
82 Thomas Jefferson and Calvin Coolidge, e.g.
83 Quiet period
84 Menial
85 Showstopper?
86 When school's open
88 More slapstick
92 Novelist McEwan
94 ___-bodied
95 Board's opposite
97 Maryland's largest city, informally
98 ___ Fisher Hall, longtime venue at Lincoln Center
99 Whale constellation
100 Capone henchman
101 Something you might get a charge out of
103 Tasty
107 "In that case . . ."
110 China's Lao-___
112 Suffered from
113 Jeff Lynne's band, for short
114 Patch of land
115 ___ season

by Alan Arbesfeld

ACROSS

1 Congratulatory gestures
10 First female U.S. solicitor general, 2009
15 Showed no moderation
16 Start of a three-part claim
17 Means of looking above and beyond
18 One may keep a watch on you
19 Esposas: Abbr.
20 "I ___ it!"
21 Kind of tea used medicinally
22 Penultimate letters
23 It doesn't have much music nowadays
24 Ritter's co-star on TV's "8 Simple Rules"
28 Fair
30 Some joeys
32 Go back and forth
37 2003 top 5 hit for Fabolous
39 Gem City of the Plains
40 Bad case of the blues
42 Title flora in a Whitman poem
43 Gallimaufries
45 Something to live by
46 Ring fingerers?
50 9-Down bits
52 Patent
53 Club collection
54 One guarded in soccer
58 Awards for romances
59 One way to sleep
61 Spasibo : Russian :: ___ : French
62 Top form?
63 Shook, maybe
64 Celebratory gesture

DOWN

1 Moves energetically
2 More than suggest
3 Star of "Scott Pilgrim vs. the World," 2010
4 Kardashians' mom
5 '60s strikers
6 Punishment, metaphorically
7 Dreamboat
8 Interjects
9 Olla, e.g.
10 Old sitcom retort
11 Got on it
12 Adorned, to a chef
13 It has a range of ranges
14 It's west of Sikkim
22 Work together closely but covertly

23 Record of the year
24 Freight platform
25 Sterling
26 Airport assignment
27 Catawampus
29 Scratch
31 Persons
33 Not at all bright
34 Member of the 1990s Persian Gulf war coalition
35 "Sweet!"
36 Feat
38 A single opening?
41 Flooring delivery
44 Be ready to explode
46 Ibsen play parodying an opera
47 "___ From the Bridge"
48 In again
49 First-rate
51 Remains on a mantel, maybe
53 Oreo component

54 Brush-off
55 "Anywhere, Anytime" sloganeer
56 The same, to Caesar
57 Spring's opposite
60 Setting for home games of the O's

by Ned White

ACROSS

1 White's partner
6 Religious journey
9 Queen's attendant
12 Treasonous groups
18 Home of Faa'a International Airport
19 Kindle, e.g.
21 Union union
22 Asian wild ass
23 1/100 of a peseta
24 With formal properness
25 Some Halloween decorations
26 Kit ___ bar
28 "Leave!"
29 Book that needs to be read word for word?
30 Picking up strength, for short?
31 Sony video recorder
33 Relatively recent
35 Postal abbr.
36 101, say
37 Corporate department
38 Party time, for short
42 7/11 product?
45 Crime of those in Dante's second circle
46 When repeated, classic song with the lyric "Sayin' we gotta go, yeah yeah yeah yeah"
47 Bully, at times
49 Begin's opposite?
51 Word of regret
53 "So what?"
55 One who aims to hit singles?
57 Quarters of a Quarter Pounder
58 Walk quietly
59 Keepers of appointments, for short
61 Deficit, informally
62 Went (for)
63 Scoundrel
65 Baseball V.I.P.s
67 Gist
68 Crucial
69 Ayatollah's speech
71 Afflicts
73 Hist. or Eng.
75 Flee
78 Ne'er-do-wells
79 In good ___
81 Twilight, poetically
84 It could go either way
86 Adhered (to)
88 Amaretto ingredients
89 Best-selling children's series "___ Jackson & the Olympians"
90 Common address start
92 Bugs someone?
94 See 97-Across
95 Explorer Meriwether ___
96 ___-breath
97 Japanese 94-Across
100 Claymation dog
102 Helpful household pets
104 Cut (off)
105 Appraises
108 Some 99-Down
110 ___ Period (part of Japanese history)
111 ___ regni
112 Go by
113 Lightly pound
115 Coming or going, say
117 Moderate
118 "No, you really must!"
119 Takes marks off
120 Yellow-and-white flowers
121 Prefix with system

122 Letters in the Greek spelling of "Parthenon"
123 Capital on the Atlantic

DOWN

1 Least mad
2 Example from classic American literature
3 Lively dances
4 Polished off
5 Example from television
6 Property unit
7 "___ you even listening?"
8 With 18-Down, structure that gets less stable with time
9 Deuce precede, maybe
10 Example from sci-fi literature
11 Brick worker's tools
12 Summer pants
13 Big dos
14 Example from 18th-century history
15 Top
16 Pleasant inflection
17 Some beans
18 See 8-Down
20 Bond holder?
27 Clad
31 Flora and fauna
32 Deceives
34 Dampens

37 Affix carelessly
39 ___ de leche
40 Cooperated with
41 Up side?
43 Duke rival, for short
44 Game center?
46 Watchmaker's tool
47 County div.
48 "I got it!"
50 "I *finally* got it!"
52 Example from fantasy literature
54 Some trilogies
56 Get running smoothly, in a way
60 Example from 20th-century history
63 Example from advertising
64 Words before a date
66 Is out
69 Point of sharpest vision
70 Golden ___
72 Cut (off)
74 Told
75 Metaphorical example from poetry
76 As well as
77 Classic roadsters
78 "One . . . two . . . three . . . ," in a gym
80 On the left, for short
82 Get together
83 Many a fed. holiday
85 British Invasion band

87 Kind of ceiling
91 Much-vilified food
93 Some fingerprints
95 Schlemiels
98 Louse's place, in Robert Burns's "To a Louse"
99 See 108-Across
101 Watch over
102 Fearsome birds
103 Welcome, perhaps
105 Ixnay
106 "A Clockwork Orange" protagonist
107 Unbelievable, say
109 Talking during a movie, e.g.
111 ___ League
114 Michigan rival, for short
116 Post-Civil War Reconstruction, e.g.

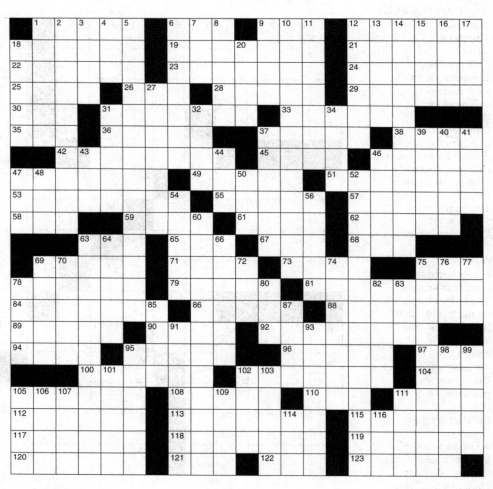

by Tom McCoy

ACROSS

1 Rule ending in 1947
4 Sharp
11 Whammy
14 Chief John Duncan, e.g.
15 Port alternative
16 Jungle swinger?
17 Opportune
18 Like many 911 calls
19 "Under a Glass Bell" writer
20 Blueprint additions
22 Corroborated
24 Renowned 1920s raider
26 Having five sharps
27 Wind up with
28 Firm cheese?
30 Borrowing bargains
39 What parades may necessitate
40 Chicken preference?
41 Counter intelligence?
42 On no occasions, to Nietzsche
43 1990s collectible
44 Move like a fly
46 Respectful appeal
52 Meets
55 Daphne du Maurier, e.g.
56 D.C.-based news inits.
57 Japanese for "finger pressure"
59 Word on two Monopoly squares
60 "Love, ___" (1979 Bel Kaufman novel)
61 General store?
62 Cause of a new wrinkle
63 Female hamster
64 Flower parts that open to release their contents
65 It's "sim" in São Paulo

DOWN

1 Mauritian money
2 One bit
3 54-Down's co-star in "The Forbidden Kingdom"
4 Big letters in bowling alleys
5 One getting the show on the road?
6 Computer hookup?
7 Checks for letters
8 Falls for it
9 Flag in a garden
10 Some xerophiles
11 Like some rugs and egg whites
12 Go
13 Prefix with phobia

21 Elizabeth Barrett Browning and Edna St. Vincent Millay, notably
23 Buoyed
25 Fitting entertainment at an arcade?
29 Leader for a time?
30 Cops
31 Allegheny River city
32 Boardwalk cooler
33 Sign of destitution
34 Headwinds often push them back, briefly
35 Bandar ___ Begawan (Brunei's capital)
36 Guard dog's quarry
37 Sources of some state funds
38 They got grounded after streaking
45 He struck Caesar "like a cur"

46 Dead-tree
47 Antipathetic
48 Perfume providing an accent?
49 Food on a stick
50 Something to upload or uphold
51 Cats with very fine short fur
52 Recalled not fondly
53 Planning
54 See 3-Down
58 Little ___

by Martin Ashwood-Smith

ACROSS

1 Crime lab tool
5 Canyon creator
8 Record number, for short
11 Butler who was a professional gambler
16 Muchacha
17 Baseball family name
18 Paris accord?
19 The works?
20 Rolls up the sleeves and begins
21 Hard-to-digest food items, in slang
23 Fruit in some Asian salads
24 "Gotcha, dude"
25 Eponym of a European capital
26 Prototype detail, briefly
28 One of 21 on a die
29 Opposition call
30 Great Lakes mnemonic
32 Ohio college named after an ancient capital
34 Letter that rhymes with three other letters
35 Musician who cofounded Nutopia
36 Tournament type
37 Something to hold money in
38 Warning to a coder
40 Alternative media magazine founder
42 Corral
44 Whoop
45 Finn's friend
47 Musical anagram of AGRA, fittingly
48 Nile biter
50 Like an unbrushed suit, maybe
51 One logging in
52 Golden ___
54 Skype annoyance
56 Something to get your mitts on?
58 Big name in lean dieting
60 Stuffed
62 Places to meditate
66 Hightail it
67 ___ Spring
69 Landing place on a bay, for short
70 "99 Luftballons" pop group
71 Seville cheer
72 "Couldn't handle the pressure, man"
74 Young Clark Kent, e.g.
76 Title in "Monty Python and the Holy Grail"
78 Bill : William :: ___ : José
79 Skater Midori
80 Wasn't square
82 Cut, in a way
83 Leans
86 P.D. broadcast
88 Cry for attention, maybe
90 Roald Dahl won three of these
92 Nail a test
93 Team leader
95 Nile biter, for short
96 Extract by percolation
97 Eyes for emotions
98 Owner of StubHub
100 Spa specialty, for short
103 A.C.A. part
104 Environmental terrorism
106 Is an ass?
107 Language along the Mekong
108 Flight
109 Soap brand with cocoa butter
110 Mustier
112 Cable, e.g.
114 Not digital
116 Do something extravagantly
118 Delight
119 Policy on some cruises
120 Slice of history
121 Base 10?
122 X-O-X line in tic-tac-toe, e.g.
123 Monopoly holdings

124 Photog's choice
125 Broadcast inits. since April 1971
126 Gifts often received while bowing the head

DOWN

1 One with spirit?
2 Postcard message
3 ___ palm
4 Line in Gotham
5 Beverage brewed without barley or wheat
6 Ones found in the closet?
7 Die, say
8 Have a heart-to-heart with?
9 Local, e.g.
10 Mercury had 26 of them
11 Becomes an adult
12 Drill sergeant's bark
13 First lady of the 1940s–'50s
14 Experiment with something
15 Sons of Liberty gathering
16 Uniform material
17 Peak performance, informally
19 Grp. that knows the drill?
22 How things may be rated
27 [Wham!]
31 Setting for a Marx Brothers farce
33 Priority system
37 Class with a Classics unit: Abbr.

39 Where to see the horn of Africa?
41 Model Banks
43 Tombstone lawman
45 ___ bar
46 Certain gelatin
49 Tattooed toon
53 Top-notch
55 Supercollider bit
57 Moving vehicle
59 Wins
61 Future atty's challenge
63 "Follow my command!"
64 Horatio who wrote the Tattered Tom series
65 Progenitors
68 Street cred
70 "What was I talking about before?"
73 ___ nerve
74 Bone whose name means "clasp" in Latin
75 Big-eyed Betty
77 "I hate the Moor" speaker
81 Go downhill
83 Dreamworld
84 Winter race vehicle
85 Next one in a row
87 Some young colleagues
89 Raised railroads
91 Drought
94 Bright spot?
97 Drawback

99 They're raised by farmers
101 Eye-openers, of a sort
102 Charge at the door, informally
105 Gear parts
106 Softly hit fly
111 Memo abbr.
113 Palliative plant
115 Hat, informally
117 Magic, on scoreboards

by Jeff Chen

ACROSS

1 Put one's shoes on?
5 Popular Mexican resort, for short
9 Convenient return option
14 Bunker implement
15 Like neatniks and clean freaks
16 Neither stood out nor bombed out
17 Refreshment on a scorching hot day
20 ". . . and that's no joke!"
21 Custom finish?
22 Portuguese explorer Bartolomeu who found a sailing route around Africa
23 Maltese, e.g.
27 Some dropped tabs
28 Athletic unit
30 "Singin' in the Rain" role
31 Alley with a time machine
33 It runs to the right
35 Aaron ___, "Thank You for Smoking" star
39 Graham ___ (old Kellogg's cereal)
40 Their 1982 album "Combat Rock" went double-platinum
42 Rod and Todd's dad, in TV cartoondom
43 Quick move?
44 Classic 1950 book with the line "It's your fiction that interests me. Your studies of the interplay of human motives and emotion"
47 Entrées
50 Linguistic root
52 Put on
53 Foreign state with the capital Panaji
54 Beatles song in which no Beatle plays an instrument
57 "Yes, let's!"
60 Emperor crowned in 962
61 "A touch more" sloganeer
62 Actress Ward
63 "Gigi" composer
64 ___ Martin
65 Alternative to Beauvais-Tillé

DOWN

1 Kind of council
2 Meet people
3 All right, to 42-Across
4 Liter lead-in
5 "Institutes of the Christian Religion" writer
6 Like the spectacled bear
7 It's easy to do for an angel
8 Some pats
9 Horticultural problem
10 With 12-Down, poker target
11 Massachusetts' Mount ___ College
12 See 10-Down
13 Squeeze
18 Like some unhealthy attachments
19 Base
24 "Boogie Nights" persona played by Mark Wahlberg
25 Able to see through
26 The out crowd?
29 Big Japanese chip maker
32 "Puh-lease!"
34 Metal band with the 1994 #1 album "Far Beyond Driven"
35 Being abroad
36 1980s baseball star Lemon
37 "Phantom Lady" co-star, 1944
38 Original D&D co.
41 "Isn't that special!"
45 "Hawaii Five-O" imperative
46 Model in a science class
48 Cricket infraction
49 Pass on a proposal
51 Checker piece, e.g.
55 Subject of a 1989 E.P.A. ban
56 ___ jure
57 Step on a scale
58 Great Plains native
59 Great Basin native

by Damon J. Gulczynski

ACROSS

1 Penny-pinching
6 Place of business: Abbr.
9 Shoot the breeze
13 Mini revelation?
18 Requests a table for one, say
20 Company behind the Hula-Hoop craze
21 Source of the line "They have sown the wind, and they shall reap the whirlwind"
22 Private things that are embarrassing
23 Moving in a nice way
25 Hungarian city
26 Not caged
28 Things in cages
29 Regarding
31 Mal de ___ (French woe)
32 Pulitzer winner for "Seascape"
34 Mystifying Geller
37 Canine command
39 Get hitched
41 Disagreement
45 Actress Elke
47 Stuck, after "in"
49 Three Stooges laugh sound
51 Prefix with -morphism
52 How some stocks are sold
53 A piano has 36 of them
55 Inverse trig function
57 Friendly
59 Warning just before a cutoff of service
62 Misdo something
63 Some grillings
64 Quick cut
65 Hair option
66 Was unfaithful
69 Bit of exercise, in Britain
72 Iranian pilgrimage city
73 Aid to Zen meditation
76 Flavor
78 Title TV character who was over 200 years old
80 Celebratory event for a new company or product
83 Venus
86 Shakespearean king
87 Changes the placement of in a tournament bracket
89 Neutral shade
90 Indian bread
91 Long-tailed monkey
94 That girl, in Genoa
95 Tell on
96 Graduation V.I.P.
97 Ewe two?
99 Yew, too
101 Atari 7800 competitor, briefly
102 Bridge writer Charles
105 Life ___ know it
107 Scruggs on a banjo
109 Bass role in a Gilbert & Sullivan opera
112 Order at a Mexican grill
115 Product with a Lubristrip
119 Plus-size model?
121 Hard evidence a lawyer follows
123 Kind of pain
124 Prisoners' wear
125 Hammed it up
126 Investigation
127 Whups
128 Something grown - or eaten - in rows
129 Powerhouse in African soccer

DOWN

1 Give up
2 Secretary of state under Reagan
3 Peut-___ (perhaps: Fr.)
4 Stars, in a motto
5 One way to complete an online purchase
6 "Candle in the Wind" dedicatee
7 Place for a brace
8 Part of a platform
9 Number two of 43
10 Den ___ (home of the International Criminal Court)
11 "Let's do this thing"
12 Later
13 Sharp pain
14 Old man?
15 Mideast grp.
16 Hat tipper, maybe
17 Some Halloween costumes
19 Ending with shop or weight
20 Question ending a riddle
24 Hedge fund pro
27 Smooths over
30 Princess of Power
33 Pro wrestler Albano
34 What an electric meter measures
35 Fans have them
36 Certain trade barrier
38 Many a Seeing Eye dog
40 Living ___
42 Sly suggestion
43 Initialism on a bank door
44 Muscle ___
46 Lunatic
48 Follower of 21-Across
50 Big brand of dog food
53 Largest coastal city between San Francisco and Portland
54 Poor grades
56 Holds up
58 Hula-Hoop, e.g.
60 Went for, puppy-style
61 They come with strings attached
67 Drinking now, paying later
68 Some movie theaters
70 "___ tu" (Verdi aria)
71 One of 10 in Exodus
74 Sunlit spaces
75 Big name in antiscience debunking
76 Fluctuates wildly
77 Greetings of old
79 Bars of music?
80 Pie crust ingredient, maybe
81 Staple of skin care
82 Asian stew often eaten with a dipping sauce
84 Pro hoopster
85 "Go" preceder
88 TV units
92 "May ___ frank?"
93 Bit of fanfare
95 Kindle, e.g.
98 ___ Rebellion (event of 1676)
100 Farm machine
103 "Swan Lake" figure
104 Milne young 'un
106 Author of "MS. Found in a Bottle," for short
108 Conifer that loses its leaves in the fall
109 Window sticker fig.
110 "Click ___ ticket"
111 Floor
113 Ancient Greek contest
114 Coulee's contents
116 "S'long"
117 "De ___" ("You're welcome": Fr.)
118 Gershwin portrayer in "Rhapsody in Blue"
120 Dunderhead
122 Motley

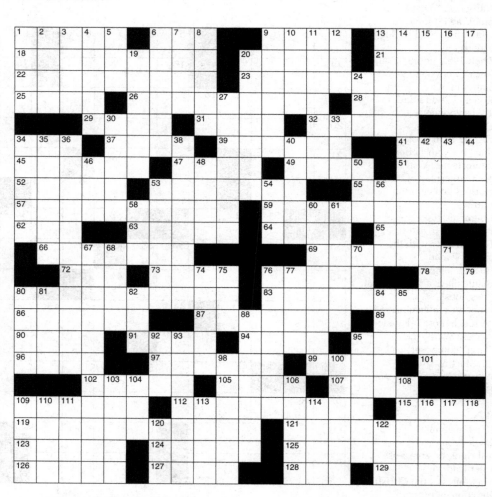

by Don Gagliardo and Zhouqin Burnikel

ACROSS

1 Leader in electronic music with multiple Grammys
9 Elks and others
15 1960s–'70s band that took its name from an Aldous Huxley title
16 Temporarily
17 Golden age for voice acting
18 Gourmet
19 Green-lit
20 Sound of an arrow being shot
22 Henry __
23 Henry __
25 Wound up
27 Computer part
28 Bar
30 One who may give you his heart?
32 Brand name with ⅔ capital letters in its logo
33 Org. with many magazines
35 Capture-the-flag game
37 Space racers
41 Like some unions
42 2000 film set in France that was nominated for five Academy Awards
44 Literary inits.
45 First name in Objectivism
46 __ Games
48 Leonine : lion :: lutrine : __
52 Secretary of energy under Clinton
54 Leaves on the side?
56 They're often blitzed
57 Internet statistic
59 Parcel
61 Alma mater for Benjamin Netanyahu
62 Composer György whose music was featured in Kubrick films
64 "It's not my place to decide"
66 Marketing space
67 Never topped
68 Group with the motto "Service Above Self"
69 17-time All-Star of the 1960s–'80s

DOWN

1 Put in effort
2 Some business casual attire
3 Website with "Ask Me Anything" interviews
4 First name in infamy
5 Boodle
6 High-end fashion brand
7 Mailing a letter, perhaps
8 Chalk talk symbols
9 Cockeyed
10 Place for a dish
11 Wilt
12 Notable features of David Foster Wallace books
13 Possible effect of doping
14 Uncomfortably tight spot, informally
21 Sign on a saloon door
24 Kind of bond
26 Headgear for Eminem
29 Awaiting a sex change, say
31 Reckless tough guy
34 Global superpower?
36 Checks
37 Religious garment suspended from the shoulders
38 Emphatic rebuttal
39 Author who created the fatalistic optometrist Billy Pilgrim
40 Unesco World Heritage Site on the Arabian Peninsula
43 Count
47 Danson's role on "Cheers"
49 Shade of red
50 Most plentiful pieces in a certain board game
51 Bonus round freebies on "Wheel of Fortune"
53 "In the __" (Nixon memoir)
55 "The beacon of the wise," per Shakespeare
58 Get moving
60 Ring bearer
63 Plural suffix
65 Mini, e.g.

by James Mulhern

ACROSS

1 Rye, N.Y., or Fort Lee, N.J.
7 Like some photographs and cliffs
13 Bouquet tossers
19 Means of access
20 Viola's love in "Twelfth Night"
21 Tombstone material
22 Wordlessly indicated "uh-oh"
23 Valiant attempt to finish off a seven-course meal?
25 ___ gel
26 Forestall, with "off"
28 Mauna ___
29 Minerals to be processed
30 What an investor in golf courses might buy?
32 Beat soundly
35 Look for
36 Grazing in a meadow and jumping fences, for two?
41 Include surreptitiously, in a way
44 Vacation unit, often
46 H of antiquity
47 Cybertrade
48 "Be sure to lose!"?
55 Org. of concern to Edward Snowden
56 Like some communities
57 ___ bone (U-shaped bone above the larynx)
58 Big small screen
61 Pac-12 team
62 Jazzmen
63 Modest hacienda
64 Two blender settings?
68 Dojo Mart, e.g.?
72 Hunting milieu
73 Dismounted
74 Audiophile's preference, maybe
75 Hone
78 Caesar's dressing?
80 Rendezvoused
81 Acting as a group
82 What I unexpectedly had for breakfast?
86 Another time
89 Toothpaste brand
90 Obstacle for a golfer
91 2012 Mark Wahlberg comedy
92 Swamp fever?
97 Doesn't keep up
99 Oxford institution
100 Floating casinos?
106 See 108-Down
109 Face value, in blackjack
110 Relative of cerulean
111 Deep South delicacy
112 Reviewer of the paperwork?
117 "Don't get yourself worked up"
119 Chow
120 Be in the offing
121 Vic with the 1949 #1 hit "You're Breaking My Heart"
122 Fraud
123 Compact containers
124 Like cherry-picked data

DOWN

1 "Sons of Anarchy" actress Katey
2 It's down in the mouth
3 Not on deck, say
4 Releases
5 Repentant feeling
6 Sleep on it
7 Green energy option
8 Fancy
9 Size up
10 English ___
11 Discontinue
12 "How ___ look?"
13 What runners may run out of
14 W.W. II "Dambusters," for short
15 About to be read the riot act
16 New Look pioneer
17 Raison d'___
18 Match makers?
21 Dead man walking?
24 Indicator of freshness?
27 ". . . the Lord ___ away"
31 Did some surgical work
32 They rarely have surnames
33 Mother of Levi and Judah
34 Poetic preposition
37 Flip response?
38 ___ Del Rey, singer with the 2014 #1 album "Ultraviolence"
39 Errand-running aid
40 Pole, e.g.
41 "Dagnabbit!"
42 Raccoonlike animal
43 Nail-care brand
45 Ring alternatives
49 Worrier's farewell
50 Mock tribute
51 ___ honors
52 Painter of illusions
53 Arm twister's need?
54 Boor's lack
59 ___-devil
60 Dancer in a pit
63 Unfair?
65 "___ fair!"
66 One to beat
67 Preprandial reading
68 Supermodel Heidi
69 Bandleader's shout
70 Good to have around
71 Added after a silence, with "up"
73 They make up everything
75 Fire extinguisher output
76 "Young Frankenstein" character
77 ___ East
79 Permanent thing
80 Some digital videos, briefly
83 Franz's partner in old "S.N.L." sketches
84 Rackful in a closet
85 Hits back?
87 Single out
88 Org. of the Jets and the Flyers
93 Occupation
94 Church chorus
95 Roars
96 Outpourings
98 "Prove it!"
101 UV light blocker
102 Residents of a certain -stan
103 "You already said that!"
104 Lying flat
105 Cut
106 Be a polite invitee
107 Mississippi River's largest tributary
108 With 106-Across, "It's time to do this thing"
113 Kind of season
114 Die spot
115 ___ oil (Australian folk medicine)
116 E.M.S. technique
118 Wine barrel wood

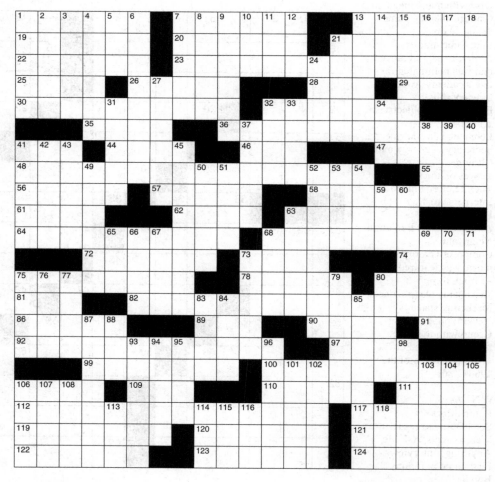

by Patrick Berry

ACROSS

1 Socialite who wrote "How to Catch a Man, How to Keep a Man, How to Get Rid of a Man"
6 It's slippery when wet
10 Acquired wisdom, per a saying
14 In ___ diagnosis
15 Zero-compromise
17 Computer data structure
18 Didn't stay secret
19 Image on Mississippi's state quarter
21 Edward Snowden, notably
22 Imitated a straining weightlifter
24 Like many stoves: Abbr.
25 Series of unknown challenges?
29 Ending for the most part?
30 Some cable splitters
31 "Approved," e.g.
33 Labrador Sea sights
34 Highland games gear
37 Thou
40 Drawing people
42 U.S.C.G. rank
44 Evacuation location
46 Hoops division
48 Divorced title couple of film
49 Acting as sentry
51 Exhibitionists?
55 1970s–'80s sitcom locale
57 Itch for
58 When a daily run starts
59 Jointly attacked?
60 Old German duchy name
61 Reason to use the 44-Across: Abbr.
62 Ones in bondage

DOWN

1 Where Chamorro is spoken
2 Blade handle?
3 "Lulu" opera composer
4 2003 N.C.A.A. hoops champs
5 Subject of the 2013 musical biography "Rhapsody in Black"
6 Seat of Monterey County, Calif.
7 6-Across ingredient
8 Mimicking
9 Nudged
10 "Pretty in Pink" heroine
11 Corporate headquarters in Mountain View, Calif.
12 Hardens
13 Pick up
16 Acronym associated with retirement?
20 Attraction
23 George Strait's "All My ___ Live in Texas"
25 A little ruff
26 Alternative to :-)
27 Vast number
28 Skedaddle
32 Turning 50, e.g.
35 Prefix with axial
36 Retired runway model
38 Meteorite impact product
39 Place for a decorative clip
40 Less outgoing
41 ___ name
42 Doesn't eat daintily
43 Sandwich chain
45 Flower-bearing shoot
47 Best Musical after "The Lion King"
50 Org. with buttons that said "There's a change gonna come"
52 In preference to
53 The Keys, essentially
54 Rule book contents: Abbr.
56 Math-based game

by Barry C. Silk

ACROSS

1 Schnozzolas
6 More reserved
11 Mali, mostly
17 Variety of primrose
18 New York Giants founder who's in the Pro Football Hall of Fame
20 Jacks or better, say, in poker
22 Philadelphia's ___ Ross Bridge
23 Arctic hideaway?
25 Take for a ride
26 Higgledy-piggledy
27 Nonviolent protests
28 Mother of Hermes
29 Strikes
32 R&B's Peniston
33 Restrained
34 Neck-stretching yoga position?
37 Haymakers?
38 Constellation next to Scorpius
39 Hound
40 Many a candidate, briefly
41 Hersey novel setting
43 Took over
45 Big win for a prominent TV financial adviser?
51 Where Bill and Hillary Clinton met, briefly
52 ___ Domenici, longtime New Mexico senator
54 Benefit offsetter
55 Old carrier name
56 ___ score (newborn health measure)
58 Original Beatles bassist Sutcliffe
59 Padre's hermano
61 Something a GPS recalculates: Abbr.
62 Monk's hood
65 Like makers of one-way street signs?
69 High point
70 Exclamation accented on the second syllable
71 Entry-level position, for short?
72 High-level, as a farm team
73 Bit of folk wisdom
75 Parts of a kingdom
77 Thai money
79 Certain bond, for short
81 Hardly Mr. Right
85 Environmentalists' concern in northern France?
88 Classic joke target
89 Either half of a diphthong
90 1970s sitcom production co.
91 Eminem producer, informally
92 Dead end?
93 Descendant of a son of Noah
96 Igloo, e.g.?
101 Milton who led Uganda to independence
102 "The race ___ !"
103 Melees
104 State that borders three Can. provinces
105 Locale of a 1984 industrial disaster
107 Shuffle, e.g.
108 Lend, slangily
111 One sending money from France or Germany?
114 Bayer brand
115 Winter vehicle
116 Sneak previews
117 Roman harvest goddess
118 Completely strip
119 Starting words of some 120-Across
120 See 119-Across

DOWN

1 Some haircuts
2 C.O.O., e.g.
3 Communion spot
4 Fate
5 Sleeper, maybe
6 Takes part in a joint session?
7 Kaiser, e.g., for short
8 Jabbers
9 Beethoven's Third
10 Whitewater enthusiast
11 Herr's heirs?
12 Humans' cousins
13 Brooder
14 Irregular
15 Adjust at Moody's, say
16 Not so conventional
18 Petruchio's task vis-à-vis Katharina
19 ___ sense
21 Herring relatives
24 Mini mints
26 Take ___ off
30 Beautified
31 Sandpiper's domain
33 Whom the witches deem "lesser than Macbeth, and greater"
34 "Hold on there, cowboy!"
35 Domain
36 American ___
37 Shut out
42 Epitome of attention to detail
44 Passion
46 Opening on Broadway
47 One might appear next to an article
48 Tombstone figure
49 Something in a bookmarks tab
50 Image in the "Jurassic Park" logo, familiarly
52 "The Prodigal Son," for one
53 Screw up
57 Feature of the Nixon tapes
58 Wee, in Dundee
60 First lady McKinley
62 Guitar accessory
63 "What a surprise to run into you!"
64 Means
66 Island that may have an apostrophe in its name
67 Light amount?
68 Martial arts level
69 Plane-related
71 "Breakfast at Tiffany's" novelist
74 Heads of staff?
76 Archetypal postwar suburb
78 ___ Janney, four-time "West Wing" Emmy winner
79 Theme
80 Coming from out of nowhere, as an insult
82 Nourishment for a plant embryo
83 Hessian river
84 Hide-and-seek no-no
86 Be behind
87 Angel's opposite
88 Overarching
91 Looks inside a house
93 Subjects of some loans
94 Teem
95 "The Prince and the Showgirl" co-star, 1957
97 Admits
98 Canine protector
99 Bit of monkey business
100 John who founded Methodism
102 "___ to break the news . . ."
105 Little nail
106 Chinese dynasty of a thousand years ago
109 ___-ready
110 Hardy heroine
112 The Horned Frogs of the Big 12 Conf.
113 Original Dungeons & Dragons game co.
114 Berlin cry

by Dan Schoenholz

ACROSS

1 Effect of tightening an extra-tight belt, maybe
10 Grilled dish
15 Chance of getting heads on two consecutive coin flips
16 First name among 1991 divorcées
17 "Whatever"
18 Vacationing, say
19 You might live by one
20 Tool for Capt. Jack Sparrow
22 Put up with put-downs
25 Surgeon's closing line?
26 Shakes
27 Division of geology
29 Undergo change
31 Do halfheartedly
33 Photoshop range
34 Ottoman commander
37 Common cry from a younger sibling
39 S-shaped line
40 Trial and error, e.g.
42 Champion of 11-Down
44 Dish providers
46 First human character on "Sesame Street"
47 Considerably
50 It burned and crashed in 1979
52 Marine mollusk named for its earlike tentacles
54 17–24, for Miss America
56 Reagan nickname
57 San Rafael is its seat
58 Long-running show about a Time Lord
61 It was boosted by Titan
62 Opposite of bore
63 Main antagonist in Disney's "Hercules"
64 Monopoly property

DOWN

1 Like some castles and zoo exhibits
2 Disposition?
3 Diversionary tactics
4 Tootled, in a way
5 Bit of product personalization
6 Org. for Cardinals and Saints
7 __ turn (perfectly)
8 Partnership indicator
9 Sets up, informally
10 Royal who toured the U.S. in the late 1970s
11 Change of life
12 Weapon for the Caped Crusader
13 Flavorer for an espresso shot
14 Blacks out
21 Indication of a pleased palate
23 Staples staple
24 Flirted (with)
28 Port whose name means "Christmas"
30 Legal suffix
31 Female fashion faux pas
32 Hula hoop, for one
34 Even a single
35 Flips
36 Refused to yield, with "down"
38 Boo-boo
41 Home of California's National Steinbeck Center
43 Rosenfeld who wrote the best seller "Live Now, Age Later"
45 McCloud of 1970s TV's "McCloud"
47 Rulings from muftis
48 Griffin who's the only two-time Heisman winner
49 Sharpen anew
51 John's accompanier
53 Hamstrings or kneecaps
54 Asian au pair
55 Mood
59 FedEx unit: Abbr.
60 The U.S. Treasury is on its back

by Kristian House

ACROSS

1 Theater purchase: Abbr.
4 Fertility doctor's focus
8 Little sucker?
11 Mountain-to-mountain transport
18 Sch. with a Manchester campus
19 Apple product
20 Fail to grant, in court
21 Showed humility
22 "Spoon River Anthology" poet Edgar ___ Masters
23 California's Rancho ___
25 Appeared amazed
26 Tattler's threat
28 At a high rate
29 "___ Folks," Charles Schulz's first strip
30 Scheme
31 Visibly sad
33 Making environmentally friendly
38 No. expert
40 One in a jungle trail
41 Walk with swaying hips
43 Arduous
46 Relative of a Great Dane
47 6 letters?
48 Like cars in a used car lot
49 Source of feta cheese
51 Prominent parts
54 Put-on
55 Clinton secretary of state
59 Ingratiate
60 Like the American pronunciation of many Polish names
62 7 1/2-foot Ming
64 Item extending over a gunwale
65 "Sesame Street" subjs.
66 An airbag can prevent it
70 Fixer-upper's need, for short
72 Counterpart of Aurora
74 Good part of a record
75 Diverge
79 Look good on
82 Citizen
84 Camera option, for short
85 She's courted in "The Courtship of Miles Standish"
88 Shipping unit: Abbr.
89 Country that's won the most medals in the history of the Winter Olympics
91 + or − thing
92 How-to aid
95 Kind of omelet
97 1990 Mike Leigh comedy/drama
100 Maven
101 First word of Dante's "Inferno"
102 "E.T." boy and others
103 "Would you let me take a look?"
106 Plagues
109 Funny
110 Coffee mate?
111 Lady in "Lady and the Tramp," e.g.
113 Fix, as a braid
117 From the top
119 Battery size
120 Put forth
121 107-Down subject
122 Org. concerned with toy safety
123 ___ Search (Bing forerunner)
124 Renaissance fair wear
125 Put on
126 Road ___
127 Where costumes are worn

DOWN

1 Dutch pot contents
2 Toll
3 1935 poem with one word per line . . . as spelled out by this puzzle's circled letters
4 Start of a reminiscence
5 Where bills may accumulate
6 Sullied
7 Extinct wingless bird
8 California's ___ Freeway
9 Common pizzeria name
10 Blue shade
11 Piece of Tin Pan Alley music
12 Midwest tribe
13 Ahab, e.g.
14 Decorative border
15 Writer of 3-Down
16 Exist
17 Pay stub abbr.
20 Remove, in a way
24 Mad magazine cartoonist Drucker
27 Like about 45% of human blood
32 Internet troll, intentionally
33 Cells that protect neurons
34 Ransack
35 In conclusion: Fr.
36 Levi's Stadium athlete, informally
37 Some Pontiacs
39 One who's much praised
42 Capt.'s inferiors
43 Clutch
44 Cause déjà vu, perhaps
45 ___ talk
46 "Family Guy" daughter
50 Certain heiress
52 ___ Period, 1603–1868
53 "___ Arizona Skies" (John Wayne movie)
56 "Just a minute," in texts
57 Cousin of an aardwolf
58 Army Rangers beret color
61 Branded footwear
63 Circle
67 Cousins
68 Ones whose work is decreasing?
69 Severe penalty
71 Harp's home key
73 Liberal arts subj.
76 Da ___, Vietnam
77 Fright wig wearer
78 Comic impressionist David
79 Lie in the hot sun
80 Thick
81 Group mailing tool
83 "31 Days of Oscar" network
85 Mound
86 Code contents
87 Barrier to some websites
90 River through Deutschland
93 What a cousin can be twice
94 Done
96 Flips
98 What may make you duck down?
99 Certain salt
100 Falafel holder
104 Steppes dwelling
105 "Beowulf" and others
107 It might have an escalator
108 Bias
110 Artist Maar depicted in Picasso's "The Weeping Woman"
112 MCAT topic: Abbr.
113 ___ room
114 Intro to biology?
115 Screen
116 Lib. listings
118 Astronomer's std.

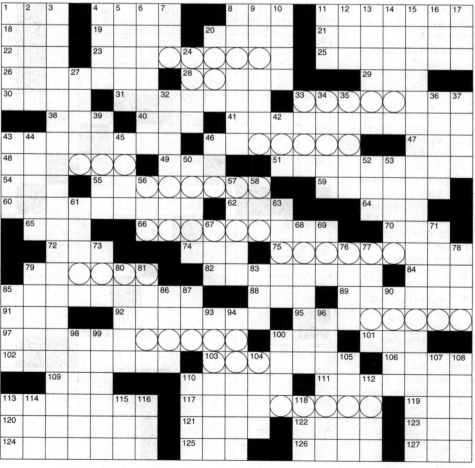

by Jacob Stulberg

ACROSS

1 Coffee-brewing device
8 "I haven't the foggiest"
15 Parole board consideration
16 Like news blogs, typically
17 Swedish university where Anders Celsius taught
18 Faulty, as a tank
19 Natural shelter
20 Hall-of-Famer with exactly 3,000 hits
21 Goddess of magic
22 Expert in calculating
23 Big Florida export
24 Sixth in a series
25 Off the ground
27 Ones skewered in P. J. O'Rourke's "Parliament of Whores"
28 Moves toward the middle
31 Children of American Communists
36 Started a movement, metaphorically
37 Barbera d' ___ (Italian wine)
41 Hole in the head
42 Former Jordanian queen
43 Exactly, informally
45 ___-com
46 Bygone Finnish coin
47 Deva, for one
49 Big name in oil
50 Poet who won three Grammys for Best Spoken Word Album
51 Tufted songbirds
52 Brush up on
53 Being tracked, in a way
54 Swore
55 Tail waggers?

DOWN

1 Highest officer in his field, ironically
2 Welcome out
3 Unsuitable for locavores
4 Tourist purchase
5 Rattle on
6 Setting for Ibsen's "Hedda Gabler"
7 Contents of some chests
8 "Isn't he great!"
9 French pioneer of sign language
10 Douglas who wrote "The Hitchhiker's Guide to the Galaxy"
11 Adopt
12 British beer with a kick
13 Bonkers
14 Tools with semicircular blades
20 What may help you hang in there?
22 Bed-hopped
25 "You ___?"
26 Some pasta
29 Languish
30 Forever stamp?
32 Secret society brother to George W. Bush and John Kerry
33 1960s–'70s detective series
34 Cheap ride
35 Group governed by the Imperial Divan
37 Note in B major but not E major
38 Rubylike gem
39 Wrestle
40 Verily
44 Place bereft of happy campers?
46 Rock: Prefix
48 Cause for an R rating
49 Lush
51 Barnyard male

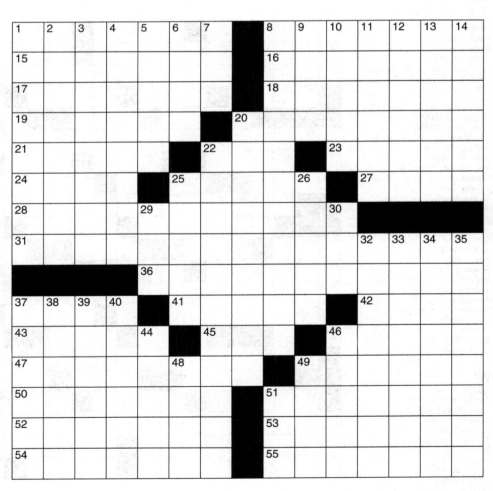

by Byron Walden

ACROSS

1 Rye and others
7 Egg-shaped tomato
11 Racetrack figure
15 A cherry may be served with it
19 Group of companies
21 Doesn't freak out
23 Set time / Go to theater / Engage in tomfoolery
25 Festive season
26 ___ Maria
27 What may follow bigger or better
28 Byways
29 "Absolutely, brother!"
31 Part of a giggle
32 Put in a hold
33 Hitchhike / Surf / Show patriotism
42 To a smaller degree
43 Dashboard abbr.
44 Meal for a seal
45 Harbor whistler
47 Good rep
48 Unshiny
50 Place to pick up prints
54 Somersault / Start football game / Invent some language
58 Not pay attention
59 Painters' picks
60 Gets established
61 Co. that produced "Lou Grant"
64 "I said ___!"
65 Nurse
66 Flashy neckwear
67 J.F.K. posting
68 Post-deluge sight
70 Shopper stopper
72 Staples of protests
75 Not stop at intersection / Warm up / Use rifle
79 Taxi's locale
80 Additions
81 "Employees must wash hands before returning to work," e.g.
84 Georgia, once: Abbr.
85 Law school accreditor, for short
86 Walton with a club
87 Diamond worker
89 Play baseball / Take public transportation downtown / Clean up after diners leave
96 Some red marks
97 Biblical preserver
98 Fudges, in a way, as an expense report
99 Earth
101 Farming prefix
103 Balkan repub.
104 Wedge or sledge
108 Finish taxes / Visit library / Plan vacation
113 Rabbit ears
114 People with belts do them
115 Dict. material
116 Tiny bit
117 Herring type
118 Pro responses

DOWN

1 3 Series producer
2 Makeup of some sheets
3 Cubemeister Rubik
4 West Wing worker
5 Forensic facilities
6 Do a darn good job?
7 Twisty pasta
8 Pod part, perhaps
9 Dashboard abbr.
10 Coordinately
11 Where I-35 and I-40 meet: Abbr.

12 Graduation ceremony V.I.P.
13 "L.A. Law" actress
14 Home of the 300 in the film "300"
15 Many a prescription?
16 Despicable one
17 A seeming eternity
18 January honoree, for short
20 Do the dishes?
22 "Austin Powers: International Man of Mystery," e.g.
24 "That was close!"
30 Iconic figure in a Warhol work
31 Seven: Prefix
32 City in 1965 headlines
33 Soft touch, for short?
34 H.M.S. part
35 Like trade-ins
36 PCs once ran on it
37 Window dressing
38 Home on high
39 Circulation needs
40 Not stiff
41 Puts the pedal to the metal
46 Davis of Hollywood
48 Showerhead adjustment
49 Diamond-loving Taylor
50 Masterstroke
51 Some printers
52 Safe place for a knife
53 Many an old monitor, in brief
55 Record of the year?

56 Go by walking
57 Top cop
61 Cohn and Chagall
62 "It is what it is," e.g.
63 "No pain, no gain," to many a bodybuilder
65 Bed support
66 Rural calls
69 ___ of hope
70 Biblical queendom
71 Steadily annoyed
72 Piece of cake
73 One left in stitches
74 Approximately, informally
76 It's a blessing
77 Chris who sang "Wicked Game"
78 Country singer Ernest
82 "U R so funny" alternative
83 Word with public or private
86 Head analysts?
87 Corrupt
88 On the line
90 Carpenter and others
91 Sizzle
92 Renaissance artist ___ del Sarto
93 Late media journalist David
94 Digital transfer
95 Peasant shoe
99 Take as a bride
100 Count of Lemony Snicket
101 ". . . ___ extra charge!"

102 Stop on the first trans-Pacific air route
103 Spelling start?
105 Lex Luthor's main henchman in "Superman"
106 Villains of fantasy
107 Facebook action
108 Busy co. around Feb. 14
109 Sinus doc
110 "So-o-o comfy!"
111 Very important
112 Remarks akin to "btw"

by Joe Krozel

ACROSS

1 Reputation ruiner
11 Some docents' degs.
15 "A likely story . . ."
16 2012 political thriller
17 Touching of noses
18 Like some Crayola crayons
19 "O Sanctissima," e.g.
20 Deep-fried pub dish
22 Not together
25 All together
26 Certain breakthroughs
28 "False, false, false!"
31 Place to build theater sets
36 Something to keep a watch on
37 ___ screen (drug test)
38 Used as a base
40 Map abbr.
41 Maude's cousin on 1970s TV
43 Certain gofer
45 "It's Not for Me to Say" crooner
47 Stumbling block
48 "My Fair Lady" lyricist
51 Swedish coins
55 Wager
58 Sushi bar supply
59 Solution for poor eyesight?
60 Form of xeriscaping
63 Certain wager
64 Night game requirement
65 Learned
66 Takes the edge off?

DOWN

1 Member of a den
2 "Slow and steady wins the race" source
3 "To the Stars" autobiographer
4 Peso spender
5 "Get ___!"
6 Overly sensitive, informally
7 Clucks
8 Power, so to speak
9 Mork's supervisor on "Mork & Mindy"
10 Words before a date
11 Ergonomics unit
12 Ascent without assistance
13 Keen
14 Part of a countdown
21 Hollowed-out comedic prop
23 County of Lewis Carroll's birth

24 One side in the annual Shrine Game
27 Wave off
29 Colon, on a test
30 Modern collection of vendors
31 ___ fields
32 Led Zeppelin's final studio album, appropriately
33 You might move over for them on the highway
34 "That's gotta hurt"
35 Some email attachments
39 Word repeated before "here," in song
42 "Friday I'm in Love" band, 1992
44 Retweeting of rave reviews, possibly
46 Gobbles
49 What fruit bats can carry
50 Drone's work, maybe

52 Gentle reminder
53 Common show time: Abbr.
54 Philippics
55 Figurehead locale
56 Founder of one of the 12 tribes of Israel
57 Having thrown in the towel, maybe
61 Natl. figure
62 Lead-in to a chef's name

by Peter Wentz

ACROSS

1 Exactly
5 Obama vis-à-vis Columbia
9 Deg. from Columbia
12 Much-anticipated nights out
20 Company with a fleet
22 Prefix with watt
23 Window shopper's cry
24 Like the roots of democracy
25 Mario's brother, in gaming
26 Breeding ground
28 Eventually became
29 Relative of a kite
30 Proofer's mark
32 "O, never say that I was false of heart . . . ," e.g.
34 "Not only that . . ."
35 Used a pouffe
36 Some spicy cuisine
37 Once, old-style
38 Competitor of Petro-Canada
40 Laura who wrote and sang "Wedding Bell Blues"
44 Join
46 "That's a ___"
48 Stuck in a mess?
50 "Ain't gonna happen"
52 Heart
54 Imminent
56 Local theater, slangily
58 Ones in an annual hunt
60 Ulan-___ (capital of a Russian republic)
61 Vehicle with a folding top
62 Suffix with stink
63 Fulda tributary
64 Jack's partner
65 Cousins
66 Goes for the gold?
67 Not quite right
69 Alternative to metal
70 Goddess in "The Tempest"
71 Win at auction, say
72 Warrior in the "Discworld" fantasy books
73 Small force
74 Form a coalition
76 Jokesters
77 Personnel list
78 ___ chi ch'uan
79 Travelers at the speed of light
80 Former Jets coach Ewbank
81 Tavern menu heading
82 One with a stiff upper lip?
83 Speed-skating champion Kramer
85 Captain's spot
87 Kind of adapter
89 Act the rat
91 It's folded before a meal
93 Dodge Aries, e.g.
95 "Walk ___" (1964 hit)
97 Red Rock dweller
99 Magazine mogul, familiarly
102 "Pretty Maids All in ___"
103 The sun's "10th planet," once
104 Half of a Senate vote
105 "This looks bad"
106 Singer ___ Rose
107 Barber's supply
108 Routine response?
109 Kyrgyz province
110 Trite
112 Needle holder
113 ___ Paradise of "On the Road"
114 Was bankrupt, say
115 Blue shade
117 Stupefy
118 Like some missed pitches
119 Stupefy
120 Baritone in "The Mikado"
121 Dyspepsia reliever
122 All at the start?
123 Home of the Big 12's Cyclones
124 One who's behind
126 Solomonic
128 ___ colada
130 Plantation machines
132 Holes in Swiss cheese

133 Grasps
135 "The Night Circus" author Morgenstern
137 Chicago mayor Emanuel
139 Yamaha Grizzly, e.g., for short
142 Trunk part
144 Pond or sand trap
146 One of the Jackson 5
147 "___-haw!"
148 Long-running event?
152 "Et voilà!"
154 One following an order
156 Countermanded
157 Verdi's "___ tu"
158 Power play result, often
159 Pope's vestment
160 They're blown at some weddings
161 Yahoo! alternative
162 Do a body scan?
163 Meanie

DOWN

1 With 141-Down, author whose work is the basis of this puzzle's theme
2 Shipmate of Spock
3 Brooklyn Heights school [U.S.; 3,9]
4 Yank
5 En route, as a tanker
6 Relaxing [U.K.; 6]
7 Host of the first World Cup, 1930: Abbr.
8 Michael of "Reservoir Dogs"
9 Spooky sounds

10 1988 Bon Jovi hit [India; 6]
11 Words said with a sigh
12 Witchy woman
13 Others, in Oaxaca
14 1996 Geena Davis thriller [China; 4,4]
15 Mountain ___ (soft drinks)
16 What chemists find attractive?
17 Cookie holder
18 "Dig in!"
19 ___-Cat
21 Leans
27 As an example
31 PBS craft show for 21 seasons [U.S.; 3,4]
33 Sci-fi narcotic
39 Military trial for a misdemeanor [India; 8]
41 "Get it?" [Japan; 8]
42 Send off
43 Popular party feature
45 Often-illegal turns, informally
47 "Hmm, gotcha"
49 Wolfe of mystery
51 Sugar suffixes
52 Benjamin
53 Mitchell heroine
55 Firehouse catching fire, e.g.
57 "Someone Like You" singer, 2011
59 Overdo it at dinner
68 Two-masted craft
73 Dr. of hip-hop
75 Ones pressed into service in the kitchen? [Egypt; 4]
76 Spitball, e.g.
77 Mens ___ (legal term)

84 Asseverate
86 Ambulance destinations, for short
88 Anatomical sac
90 Book before Esth.
91 Even often in a front yard
92 Passage between buildings
94 Stream
96 ___ Tate, onetime English poet laureate
98 Secretariat's org.
100 Send off
101 Pilots
108 One-liner, e.g.
109 Stable bagful
111 Gets broadcast
112 McGregor of "Big Fish"
116 Dream
125 A neighbor
127 "Kind of" ending
129 Rainbow color
131 "Ta-ta"
134 Lyric poem
136 Eager, informally
138 Overflow seating area
140 "Coffee, ___ Me?"
141 See 1-Down
143 Longfellow bell town
145 "Um, pardon . . ."
148 Rabble
149 A.I. woman in 2015's "Ex Machina"
150 Std.
151 Old game console inits.
153 Dress (up)
155 1990s Indian P.M.

by Kevin G. Der

ACROSS

1 It may facilitate playing with one's food
9 Like TV's Dr. Richard Kimble, famously
15 Prestige
16 Spectator who got a standing O at Wimbledon in 1981
17 Mushroom layer of a beef Wellington
18 Quintessential
19 Point made by architects
20 "Whatever the case . . ."
22 Throw a party for
23 What was due for some pioneers?
24 Like spent charcoal
25 Danger in stories of Sinbad the sailor
26 Addresses with bared teeth
29 Has things reversed, maybe
31 Where most occupants need masks, for short
32 Soft-serve ice cream requests
36 Pirates' place
38 Trademark Isaac Asimov accessory
39 Mammals that congregate in groups called "rafts"
40 Was yellow, say
41 April, May or June
42 Heads for the garden?
45 Annual Vancouver event, familiarly
46 Recipient of 11-Down
49 No. 2
50 Gets the lead out, quaintly
52 Chalked warning left for custodial staff
54 Relative position?
56 Business reply card, e.g.
57 Prone to tantrums
59 Layette item
60 Showed interest, in a way
61 Count
62 "Das Kapital" topic

DOWN

1 Footwear donned on camera by Mr. Rogers
2 Volunteer's assurance
3 Onetime Strom Thurmond designation
4 Comics pet in a horned helmet
5 Rows
6 The bigger picture: Abbr.
7 TV honor last presented in 1997
8 Newsman Holt and others
9 Noted employee of Slate
10 Salacious
11 Something shown to 46-Acrosses
12 Winged mimics
13 Mrs. Theodore Roosevelt
14 Full of risk
21 Class in which students raise their hands, briefly?
25 Overhaul
27 Really bad idea
28 Corset-making tool
30 Informal gauge of credibility
33 Where you might lose an hour
34 It might gain you an hour
35 Germ
37 It's targeted for extraction
38 Cultured ones?
40 "The Principles of Mathematics" philosopher
43 Org. conducting lots of X-rays
44 U.P.S. label phrase
46 Burn the midnight oil, e.g.
47 1959 #2 hit whose flip side was "La Bamba"
48 Earliest symptoms
51 Consign to a time capsule, say
53 New York county on the Canadian border
55 Gains a 54-Across
58 Kind of port

by Samuel A. Donaldson and Brad Wilber

ACROSS

1 Choco ___ (Klondike treat)
5 School
10 Items that may be labeled SMTWTFS
15 Dog sound
18 Series of numbers?
20 Kurt Vonnegut's "Happy Birthday, ___ June"
21 Former part of the British Empire
22 Joe Biden's home: Abbr.
23 "I expected as much"
25 Towering
26 Letters of obligation
27 Hair piece
28 Currency which, in one denomination, features a portrait of Linnaeus
30 Garment for tennis, perhaps
32 Not as exciting
34 Return from a store
37 When blacksmithing began
39 Perfect orbit
40 Fanatical
41 66, e.g.: Abbr.
42 Nav. rank
43 Run ___
44 Boarded
45 "Awe-SOME!"
47 Occurring in March and September, say
50 Shenanigans
53 Dietary no-no
54 Grey and ochre
55 "There is ___ in team"
56 Pleasant inflection
57 Park opened in 1964
59 Easy-peasy task
60 Chocolate mint brand with peaks in its logo
63 Temperature units
64 Muscles worked by leg presses
65 Anti-Revolutionary of 1776
66 Gets harsher
68 An example of itself
70 Lacto-___ vegetarian
71 Condemned
72 Gone
76 Hockey team with a patriotic name
78 Distraction for many an idle person
80 Bests
81 Capacious
82 Apple desktop
83 National Novel Writing Mo.
84 Havana-to-Palm Beach dir.
85 Eagerly accept
86 See 92-Across
88 Handled roughly
90 Japanese for "teacher"
91 Message to one's followers
92 Portrayer of 86-Across in "Elf"
93 Artifact
95 Rakes
97 Cooking spray brand
98 "The Downeaster '___'" (Billy Joel song)
100 Sleep mode?
106 Malt product
107 Bring home the gold
108 Barely manage
109 Breakfast cereal maker
110 Hyphenated fig.
111 Factions
112 "It was just a joke!"
113 Where writing is on the wall?

DOWN

1 Mai ___
2 Bottom-row key
3 Capt. Kangaroo's network
4 Peak that's known as "The Great One"
5 Rare notes
6 Crisp bit in a stir-fry
7 Further
8 String after B
9 Seafood soup base
10 Series opener
11 Privy to
12 Attraction that operates under its own steam?
13 Not in the dark
14 Authorization
15 Catcher of some waves
16 Shake-ups in corps.
17 Champagne holder
19 Seasonal linguine topper
24 "___ even"
29 Expunge
31 Prepare to tie a shoelace, say
32 Staple of quiz bowls
33 Redolence
35 Pro ___
36 Coin to pay for passage across the River Styx
38 Put another way
39 Strewn
41 Fodder for tabloids
44 Little bugger
45 Wise ones
46 Daughter of Hyperion
48 Condition of sale
49 TV's "The ___ Today"
50 Bring, as to a repair shop
51 Thoroughfare
52 Dog sounds
54 Collapsed, with "in"
57 Ends of letters
58 Somebody ___
59 Words below an orange on a license plate
60 One of 24 in a glucose molecule
61 Bagel topper
62 It might contain a list of postal abbreviations
63 Something you might get a kick out of?
64 Steven Wright's "I intend to live forever. So far, so good," e.g.
66 Capital city founded during a gold rush
67 Mariana, e.g.
68 ___ a one
69 What's superior to Lake Superior: Abbr.
71 Hip-hop's Mos ___
72 Hematophagous creature
73 Buddy
74 Pass
75 Hand source
77 Bank to rely on
78 Soaks (up)
79 Pouting expression
81 Major stockholder?
83 "m" and "n"
85 Hula hoop?
86 Dumbfound
87 Small change
88 June honorees
89 Parts, as blinds
90 Blind parts
94 Highway number
96 Variety of antelope
99 Fiction
101 Old White House moniker
102 Unit usually seen with the prefix deci-
103 Equal: Prefix
104 Big name in current research?
105 Point of writing?

by Tom McCoy

ACROSS

1 Some safety stats: Abbr.
5 She queried a magic object named twice in this puzzle's circled squares
14 Black cats and comets
15 Vied (for)
16 Hang in the balance?
17 1980–83 Stanley Cup winners
18 Rivet
20 Cuttlefish feature
21 Less than
23 Didn't budge
24 Impassive
26 1992 Prince song or its peak position in Billboard
30 Stir stir
33 Tempestuous talent
34 In good order
35 Header on many a forwarded email
36 She may give you the coat off her back
39 Press for change?
40 Annual charge
42 Darwin's "The Descent ___"
45 Step up
47 Parts of one's inheritance
48 Pol. affiliation of British P.M. William Gladstone
50 Implores
53 Go from here to there instantly
57 Lecture
59 Heavy, durable china
61 Lorenzo's love
62 Winning line
63 Former Yankee skipper in the Hall of Fame
64 Answer provided by the magic object named twice in the circled squares
65 Bygone sticker

DOWN

1 Poker player's words of concession
2 Bête ___
3 Small tower on a castle
4 Third class on the Titanic
5 Former Big Four record company
6 Like Russia, of all countries

7 Having a day off
8 Tends (toward)
9 Longtime sponsor of the Socceroos national soccer team
10 Given the latest
11 Monthly bill: Abbr.
12 English title
13 Business page heading
14 Not be settled with
19 Many an "I Ching" user
22 Tailor's measurement
25 Annual Augusta event
27 Mood
28 Continually
29 Hounds or badgers
30 Launch locations
31 Thrash
32 International company with an acronymic name
37 John with the 1984 #1 hit "Missing You"

38 Latino star once named one of "The 10 sexiest bachelors in the world" by People magazine
41 Wrong start?
43 Words of reassurance
44 Speeding (along)
46 Shop tool
49 Mess up
51 Certain bulb component
52 Man: Prefix
53 Small songbirds
54 Home of the Lia Fáil
55 Unhinged
56 Pita-like bread
58 Former G.M. make
60 Having a large footprint?

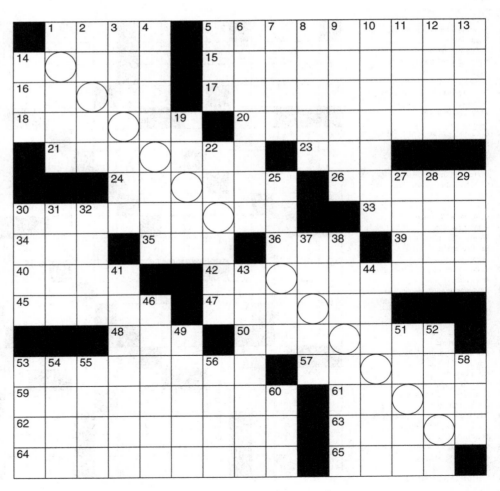

by Jason Flinn

ACROSS

1 Shopping lines?
4 Without warranty
8 Collision
14 Rolls out the green carpet?
18 Most balanced
20 Band member with a long neck
21 Curriculum component
22 "And they're off! Ace Detective has the ___!"
23 On fire
24 The titular scarlet letter
25 Pennsylvania N.L.'ers
26 Dennis who fronted the 1960s–'70s Classics IV
28 "Looks like Setting Sun is ___!"
30 Purina product line
32 Scarf (down)
34 Fissures
35 "It's Pariah ___!"
40 Associate
42 Tool made to scale
43 Ink containers for squids
44 Public venues
45 All alternative
48 Sleep: Prefix
49 Part of a Derby garland
50 Some peers
52 Abbr. after many a general's name
53 Skill tested by Zener cards
54 Rag
56 "Chiropractor heads into the ___!"
58 Fixate (on)
60 N.Z. neighbor
61 Sound you can't make in your sleep
62 Maven
64 "Here's where Mississippi Delta often ___!"
69 They tend to brood
70 Tara's owner
72 Locale of Ada and Enid: Abbr.
73 Spelling practice?
75 "Now Carrier Pigeon takes the ___!"
79 Invasive Southern plant
80 Child's medicine dose, often: Abbr.
83 Tax
84 Essential amino acid
85 Leafy vegetable
86 Words after "tough row"
88 Feedbag grain
89 Verb with "vous"
90 Hobbes's favorite food in "Calvin and Hobbes"
91 Evidence of one's upbringing
92 Calculator that doesn't shut off
95 "But wait! Amex Card ___!"
97 Show one's disapproval
99 Rockies ski resort
100 Hershey brand
101 "Almost there, and E Pluribus Unum will be ___!"
104 River islands
107 "Twelfth Night" woman
111 Remedy for a 59-Down
112 Moon of Uranus
114 "But the winner is . . . Inseam ___!"
116 Where Luang Prabang is
117 The "little blue pill"
118 Noted Moscow opening of 1990
119 Part of GPS: Abbr.
120 Stationary
121 Member of the 600 home run club
122 His or her, to Henri

DOWN

1 Deseret, today
2 Gilpin of "Frasier"
3 Dirty Harry's surname
4 Have a bug, maybe
5 "Bye for now"
6 Aoki of the World Golf Hall of Fame
7 Regs.
8 Supermarket chain
9 Smother, as sound
10 Rice dish cooked in broth
11 Barely
12 Sleeveless undergarment, for short
13 Penetrating
14 One in the pipeline?
15 In succession
16 Carried out, biblically
17 Top-three finishes and total earnings, in horse racing
18 Patriot Day's mo.
19 Ones having a rough spell?
27 How the careful think
29 Mop & ___
31 "Annabel Lee" poet
33 Takes too much, briefly
35 Seine tributary
36 Sgts. and cpls.
37 Cracker Jack prizes that leave a mark
38 2005 South African drama that won a Best Foreign Film Oscar
39 Pageant accessory
40 It's often at the end of a bottleneck
41 Suit in a Spanish card deck
44 De ___ (actual)
46 Intel mission
47 Eldest of the Three Musketeers
49 Bonheur who painted "The Horse Fair"
50 Arab city whose name is an anagram of ARABS
51 Mrs., in Madrid
55 Race segment
56 Base brass
57 Foxtrot preceder
59 Scald, e.g.
60 Words on a docent's badge
62 Reached
63 Kirk's partner in a groundbreaking 1968 interracial kiss
65 Middays
66 Anatomical danglers
67 Anatomical mass
68 Bagel shop amt.
71 C.I.O. partner
74 Thick-walled pot
76 1971 top 20 hit with no English lyrics
77 VW forerunners?
78 Rushes
79 He died at Xanadu
81 Record number?
82 N.F.L. coach Carroll
85 Ollie's partner on old children's TV
87 Simple wind instruments
90 Skater Babilonia
91 Comics "Oh no!"
93 Bidding
94 Bad "Wheel of Fortune" buy for SUSPICIOUS ACTIVITY
95 Key presenters
96 Syrian ruling family
97 Apothecary items
98 Bit of dental repair
99 Brink
102 Life lines?
103 At hand
105 Some old PCs
106 Mattel subsidiary that got its start in model trains
108 Creepy look
109 Old Fords
110 Checkup sounds
113 "The Confessions of ___ Turner" (1967 Pulitzer-winning novel)
115 Long, on Lanai

by Samuel A. Donaldson

ACROSS

1 Ultra-environmental policy
10 Desert plant pollinated by moths
15 Tiger or boa constrictor
16 Foursome in Mahler's "Symphony of a Thousand"
17 Group of practice-only N.F.L. players
18 Lead-ins to games of chicken
19 Tan and others
20 Garden ornament
21 Nickname
22 Regalia
24 Bits of baby talk
25 Source of the line "Madness in great ones must not unwatch'd go"
29 Film
31 Alert at 52-Down
32 Ray variety
33 "Putting the phone down for a sec," in textspeak
35 Sign of lycanthropy, to some
37 Comic book legend with many movie cameos
39 The anchorman in "Anchorman"
40 Are around
42 Celerity
43 It's often met "on the road taken to avoid it," per Jean de la Fontaine
45 Some summer fare
46 Went off the board
47 Where Chipotle was founded and is headquartered
49 Stop playing hide-and-seek
51 Butt
52 Engage in
56 1973 self-titled album with the #1 hits "Photograph" and "You're Sixteen"
57 Miniaturizing device in "Fantastic Voyage"
59 Script instruction
60 Criminal who welcomes a hanging?
61 When doubled, very affectionate
62 Lowest point?

DOWN

1 Riemann ___ function
2 Class act?
3 New York City theater where CinemaScope debuted
4 Big maker of moving walkways
5 Land O' Lakes land: Abbr.
6 Clear
7 Reject
8 New Jersey city that's at the terminus of Interstate 80
9 Gate fig.
10 Someone who speaks like the quote in 25-Across
11 Congo feeder
12 Julia Child, e.g.
13 Singer who was a coach on four seasons of "The Voice"
14 Twits
21 "Grand" place to stay
22 Pride : lion :: business : ___
23 Pig ___
25 Number before a colon
26 Dating standard
27 WrestleMania highlights
28 Ad follower
30 One-minute excerpt, maybe
32 Pen set
34 They're raised in some gardens
36 Lime, e.g.
38 "Latino USA" carrier
41 Mostly-women Olympics sport, familiarly
44 Suit materials
45 Pass along, with dubious propriety
46 Literature Nobelist Walcott
48 Bent for collecting curios
50 Rating an R rating, say
52 1970s–'80s sitcom locale
53 Legendary galley
54 Manxman, e.g.
55 Fictional hiree at Thornfield
57 Parent of Air Greenland
58 Theatrical form

by Brad Wilber and Doug Peterson

ACROSS

1 Theoretically, at least
8 Social exchanges
13 Creator of Stupefyin' Jones
19 It's said to be "the mother of success"
20 Offshore sight
22 Painted amateurishly
23 Dispute between Loretta Lynch and her co-workers?
25 1994 movie based on an "S.N.L." character
26 Nike competitor
27 Naval bases?
28 B'way buy
29 Manila moolah
30 Words before "Be" and "Go" in two hit songs
32 Option for a non-grad
33 Fowl pole?
35 Rank above bey
37 Army V.I.P. at a military parade?
41 Chemistry unit: Abbr.
44 System starter?
45 Early times, for short
46 "Voulez-___" ("Mamma Mia!" song)
47 Deck (out)
48 Smartest one to consider a case?
52 Ballet jumps
53 Suffix with Manhattan
54 Dreamboat
55 Org. that regulates arsenic and asbestos
56 Oscar Wilde poem "The Garden of ___"
57 Say for sure
58 "It brings tears to my eyes"
59 Loafer, e.g.
62 Winter coats
64 Municipal building located where major roads intersect?
68 The same as
71 Empty ___
72 One fry short of a Happy Meal
76 Sally ___ (sweet bun)
77 Letter from the teacher
79 Religious title
80 Became enamored with
81 Dorm V.I.P.s
82 Sprays, with "down"
83 Nun for the defense?
85 Sch. in Norfolk, Va.
86 Abbr. on a town's welcome sign
87 Dead-on
88 Attention getters
89 Dummkopf
90 G.I. dressed like a priest?
96 Exposed
97 Not look forward to at all
98 Play ___ with (harm)
99 Standard deviation symbol
103 Desiccate
105 Where It.'s at
106 Truman's Missouri birthplace
108 Third-class
109 Dick ___, Pro Football Hall of Fame coach who popularized the zone blitz
110 Felon at a campground?
113 Least active
114 In the future
115 New parent's purchase
116 Early online forum
117 Night lights
118 Lowlifes

DOWN

1 Slaughterhouse scraps
2 Green
3 Live in squalor, informally
4 Secretary of state after Ed Muskie
5 Wall Street order
6 Tenor in "The Flying Dutchman"
7 Back away from
8 Might have, informally
9 Blow off steam?
10 Flight stat.
11 Spiral seashells
12 Fed up with
13 Go for ___ (swim)
14 It might allow a student to avoid detention
15 Vituperate, informally
16 Best blood type for a transfusion recipient
17 Toy blowgun
18 Summer hours in L.A.
21 Recovers from
24 Raspberry
31 Any member of One Direction
33 Frost-covered
34 Bring forward
36 Ticks off
38 Most-watched TV series of 2012–13
39 "S.N.L." castmate of John, Dan and Gilda
40 Breakfast cereal
41 Degs. for future financiers
42 Great Seal word
43 Landlocked Asian land
49 How most Campbell's soup comes
50 Kid
51 Satellite connections
52 Longtime reality TV family on the E! channel
57 When there's "darkness" in a classic Arthur Koestler novel
60 Sleepers, for short
61 Closet collection
63 Featured musicians
65 Maximum
66 Like some peanuts and celebrities
67 Political suffix
68 Cheap smoke, in slang
69 Most mammals
70 Not appropriate
73 Home of Broken Arrow and Broken Bow: Abbr.
74 Mom-and-pop orgs.
75 Pained plaints
78 Follow-up to a cross-examination
80 1982 Disney film
82 Nut job
83 Earned a citation, maybe
84 Watches
87 It's a sin
91 Tony winner for "Pippin"
92 One making cell transmissions
93 Macbeth and Macduff
94 Where to see a van Gogh in N.Y.C.
95 What many English do in the afternoon
100 Bernhard ___, so-called "Subway Vigilante" of 1984
101 Con game
102 Song and dance, in Seville
104 Jabba, for one, in "Star Wars"
106 Portray
107 Unit of currency for some oil
109 Lucy of TV's "Elementary"
111 ___ shu pork
112 Science advocate Bill

by Randolph Ross

ACROSS

1 Be successful, well-liked, etc.
10 Brienne of ___, "Game of Thrones" protagonist
15 Glutamine, e.g.
16 Informed
17 Architectural features above arches
18 Common pie flavor
19 Lose crunchiness, as breakfast cereal
20 Speed-skating venue
21 Gently enter
22 Service begun in 1947, for short
24 Truths
26 B-school grad, perhaps
27 Rising sea levels, e.g.
29 Medical prefix with -scope
30 Level, to a Brit
31 Introductory course?
33 Like "hostess" and "comedienne"
35 Country created by the Treaty of Sèvres, 1920
37 Tesla, e.g.
38 It produces a flavorful crust on some meat
42 Interest, e.g.
45 Old Crayola color akin to Tropical Rain Forest
46 Cry
48 Bargains for time?
50 Binge
51 Have ants in one's pants
53 Untouched?
54 Subject of the campaign slogan "Fifty-four forty, or fight!"
56 Place in New York City?
58 Man's nickname composed of three Roman numerals
59 Egyptian god of war
60 Kick back while watching the ball game, say
62 Zeroes
63 Hostess offering
64 Panache
65 Social media debut of 2010

DOWN

1 "How's it goin'?"
2 Is obtrusive
3 Falls on the border
4 ___ Wilson, lead singer for Heart
5 Brouhaha
6 Woolly bear, e.g.
7 Scaling tool
8 Aid in restoring a crown
9 Some deadline setters, in brief
10 With 61-Down, grazing locale
11 Throws for a loop
12 Pit sight
13 Wander
14 Like some tattooed hands
21 Bitcoin, e.g.
23 Son- or daughter-related
25 Output of Thomas Gray
28 It's just for fun
30 Luke Skywalker and Princess Leia, e.g.
32 Capital of Australia's Northern Territory
34 Echoing sound in a cave
36 Area of study?
38 Capital of Antigua and Barbuda
39 Depart in a cloud of dust, perhaps
40 On tenterhooks
41 2013 World Series M.V.P., to fans
43 Stop troubling
44 Jack ___
47 Lighten up
49 Confidence
51 Chicago-born choreographer
52 ___ Dilfer, Super Bowl XXXV-winning QB
55 Dock figure
57 Feminist author Millett
60 Short flight
61 See 10-Down

by Kyle T. Dolan

ACROSS

1 Sunni jihadist grp.
5 -
10 Alternatively, online
14 -
19 Impermanent hill
20 Bath-loving TV character
21 Lionhearted sort
22 College booster?
23 Fuji rival
24 Ingredient in glassmaking
25 Meal plan
26 Architect of the Guggenheim Museum in Bilbao
27 Genetic variant
29 Melodramatic sound
31 What may be forever?
33 High school class, briefly
34 Exams that students get F's on?
35 Liquid harmful to vampires
37 100 Iranian dinars
38 Fully caffeinated, say
39 Stood for
40 Singer Carlisle of the Go-Go's
42 Yardbirds
43 Lexical ref.
44 Land
45 Former Seattle pro
46 Looney Tunes "devil," for short
47 -
49 Lighted icons on airplanes
53 Coming down the line?
55 -
57 Offshoot
58 Scratches (out)
59 Imaginary
61 Former Houston athlete
62 Annual celebration on January 6
65 First silent film to win Best Picture since "Wings"
68 -
69 i, for −1
70 Arch locale
71 Give a zero-star review, say
73 "Once again . . ."
75 When viewed one way
76 Opposites of fantasts
80 Piddling
82 Response deflecting blame
83 More to come shortly?
85 Magnetic induction unit
86 Org. whose website has a lot of links?
88 Poetic dusk
89 Something to take to a beach
90 English monarch called "the Magnificent"
93 Manhattan campus
95 ___ voce
96 Move like groundwater
97 The devil's workshop, as the saying goes
99 -
100 Sea dog
101 -
102 Peace, to Pushkin
103 Over again
104 Time for a siesta, perhaps
106 Boot
108 Whole essence
110 Having a row
112 Fibonacci, for one
113 Atop
114 Shark girl in "West Side Story"
115 TV amazon
116 Initiates
117 Tickled, and how!
118 Part of an unsound argument
119 As a consequence

DOWN

1 State bordering B.C.
2 Rio de Janeiro peak
3 Something caught in the air
4 Some arctic hunters
5 [Automobiles]
6 Member of a noted quintet
7 Big inits. in comedy
8 Attaches, as with rope
9 Study for a Masters?
10 One doesn't have much resistance
11 Golfers drive off it
12 Ready follower?
13 Mobile home
14 [Video games]
15 ___ kwon do
16 Garbage collector
17 Multitudinous
18 Quid pro quo on the radio
28 Young salamander
30 Small storage space
32 North-flowing English river
34 What might be revealed in silence
35 Ibsen's "___ Gabler"
36 Fresh from a shower
37 Crunchy snacks
39 Quit it
41 Mad ___

43 Gape at
45 Some offshoots
47 [Sportswear]
48 Firm, in a way
49 Step above amateur
50 Debtor's burden
51 Pamplona runner
52 Bank deposit?
54 Getting together
55 [Mattresses]
56 Fancy spread
60 Foolhardy
62 Paradoxically, when it's round it's not circular
63 Trick, slangily
64 Horse color
66 Suggestions
67 Improved, as relations
68 [Elevators]
72 Bean on the moon
74 Actress Cannon
75 Sneaky
77 Vessels near washstands
78 Lipton employee
79 Needlework
81 Book report?
82 General defeated by Scipio, ending the Second Punic War
84 Grow tiresome
86 "Balderdash!"
87 "g," to a chemist

89 Relative of a halberd
90 Prevents
91 "Hey ___" (1977 Shaun Cassidy hit)
92 Minimal
93 "Soap" spinoff
94 Glandular prefix
95 Certain 35mm camera
98 Magnifying lens
99 [Insurance]
101 [Hotels]
103 Some madrigal singers
105 Ballet step
107 Earth-shattering invention?
109 2008 bailout recipient, for short
111 Path to enlightenment

by Timothy Polin

1

```
BOTCH ▪ SEVENIRON
RHODA ▪ ALANADALE
AINTI ▪ FULLTIMER
IFY ▪ KEELS ▪▪ OBIT
NODOUBT ▪▪ BACONS
GRAY ▪▪ BYTHEBY ▪▪
AGNES ▪ BOOTY ▪ LES
MOZZARELLASTICK
ETA ▪ PILED ▪ SAVOY
▪▪▪ SOFTTOP ▪ RELY
BOGART ▪▪ NEMEROV
ORLY ▪▪ GHANA ▪ AGO
TOYSTORES ▪ REDID
HUPMOBILE ▪ TRASK
ATHEISTIC ▪ SERTA
```

2

```
JAN ▪ FBI ▪ PALM ▪ OFFISH
ANAT ▪ URN ▪ ATEAM ▪ POUNCE
COMEONIN ▪ XWORD ▪ EARTHY
OMENS ▪ NEGRO ▪ IMONLYHU
BILDUNGSRO ▪ BLASE ▪ EMI
SAYS ▪ ROSEMARY ▪ CROWBAR
▪▪ BEAU ▪ AGENDA ▪ PRANK
ASFAR ▪ THENOW ▪ ARRAIGNS
NORRIS ▪ ELA ▪ PBR ▪ ELS ▪
OHO ▪ TERRA ▪ PUREED ▪ TINA
DOYOUWANTTOBUILDASNOW
ETON ▪ SEAEAR ▪ NAMIB ▪ ATM
▪ ECU ▪ NSC ▪ ACS ▪ TALISA
CRASHPAD ▪ KISHKA ▪ CARON
AIMEE ▪ DOOLEY ▪ LAIN ▪
SCATTED ▪ TERMITES ▪ DOLL
SEZ ▪ VESTS ▪ MORGANFREE
▪ WONDERWO ▪ VENAL ▪ SODOM
LINEAR ▪ AMBIT ▪ MACARENA
SNARFS ▪ PARER ▪ PSA ▪ MAIN
DESOTO ▪ NOSY ▪ SSN ▪ LAS
```

3

```
CTEAMS ▪▪ THEMRS
ARABIAN ▪ CHEROOT
SARONGS ▪ REYNOSA
UNTO ▪ ETHAN ▪ SNIT
ASH ▪ CHAITEA ▪ LEI
LAS ▪ HERDERS ▪ ITO
TCCHEN ▪▪ VAUGHN
ITIS ▪ SWEDE ▪ THEM
EIEIO ▪ AMI ▪ TETRA
SONAR ▪ DUD ▪ ASSIN
ONT ▪ EPI ▪ IVS ▪ OVA
FDIC ▪ INICE ▪ ONEG
WASHINGTONSTATE
ATTENTIONGETTER
RESTSONONESOARS
```

4

```
JAFAR ▪ OLORD ▪ PRISM ▪ BAT
EPOCH ▪ MASAI ▪ LOTTO ▪ IDI
SHARONSTONE ▪ ASSIN ▪ ZAG
SIMONE ▪ SLOGAN ▪ PROTEGE
EDS ▪ DAS ▪ ENOSSLAUGHTER
▪▪ BATHE ▪ SHOOTPAR ▪
ESAU ▪ EAVES ▪ ENG ▪ MEWLS
BOBBYSHERMAN ▪ TOYSHOP
BARBET ▪ EOS ▪ PAAR ▪ HOPE
SPALL ▪ LOCKA ▪ OLMEC ▪ LED
▪ SYLVESTERSTALLONE ▪
PEI ▪ SEALE ▪ UHURA ▪ NOMAD
AMOS ▪ ANOD ▪ LIS ▪ ENTIRE
PENCILS ▪▪ BEVERLYSILLS
ARSON ▪ AFR ▪ ARNIE ▪ OKOK
▪ RAPSHEET ▪ ASLAN ▪
MYLESSTANDISH ▪ PIT ▪ ROO
COLDWAR ▪ LATTER ▪ FLOORS
IGA ▪ ELENA ▪ LORETTASWIT
NIM ▪ AMAIN ▪ ELOPE ▪ SHANE
GSA ▪ TSKED ▪ DENSE ▪ TANGO
```

5

```
BUFFSUP ▪ SIDEBAR
APRIORI ▪ UPCCODE
SHOGUNS ▪ BACKSUP
KELLS ▪ ASADA ▪ PLO
ERIE ▪ SNIT ▪ BOOTS
DECAMP ▪ ROK ▪ BRET
▪▪ FORCEMAJEURE
BBS ▪ LIONIZE ▪ SYD
RICHTERSCALE ▪▪
AGRO ▪ RIO ▪ KLATCH
SMACK ▪ ANKH ▪ TALE
SOB ▪ MUNGO ▪ NEPAL
HUBBARD ▪ JAINISM
ATLARGE ▪ ACCURSE
THEATER ▪ KEEPSAT
```

6

```
BOSS ▪ STEAM ▪ CHOP ▪ ADREP
OATH ▪ TURBO ▪ LULU ▪ DEANE
THAI ▪ ANTED ▪ OLIN ▪ UPFOR
HUGELUGELUGSLOGSLOTS ▪
▪ LOBO ▪ LIE ▪ EATS ▪
MAIDSAIDSANDSANKSINK
ISL ▪ CLEATS ▪ ANTI ▪ TOUR
SCOTCH ▪ CEE ▪ VAN ▪ ONE
CANAL ▪ SAN ▪ RIBALD ▪ ASIF
▪ PALEPALSPASSLASSLESS
ERAS ▪ RTE ▪ SCAM
KIDSKISSMISSMOSSMOST
ODIE ▪ DYNAMO ▪ ANO ▪ ONION
NED ▪▪ ADO ▪ LYE ▪ BADDIE
GASP ▪ ALFA ▪ NONAME ▪ ELS
▪ LOUDLOUTLOSTLASTCAST
▪ LUAU ▪ ETA ▪ CIAO ▪
▪ WILTWILLFILLFULLFUEL
HANOI ▪ SEAT ▪ TEASE ▪ FOXY
ONCUE ▪ CAMI ▪ OAKEN ▪ IMAM
PEATS ▪ KHAN ▪ SNERT ▪ NOME
```

7

```
B Y G O S H · A W E · A N T S
L E A N T O · L E T S D O I T
U N I C U M · A L H A M B R A
S T U D D E D · D E F I L E R
H A S · I M E D · L E X E M E
· · L O A V E S · · F A A ·
· L O S T O N E S S H I R T ·
· D E T E C T I V E W O R K ·
· K I D S T H E S E D A Y S ·
E V A · · S O N A N T · · ·
N E S T L E · N U T S · U T A
T I T H I N G · P I N E S O L
I N R E V O L T · V E L U R E
S T A T E L A W · E C L A I R
H O Y A · A D O · S K Y L I T
```

8

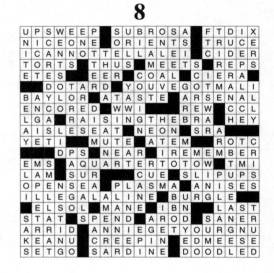

```
U P S W E E P · S U B R O S A · F T D I X
N I C E O N E · O R I E N T S · T R U C E
I C A N N O T T E L L A L E I · C I D E R
T O R T S · T H U S · M E E T S · R E P S
E T E S · E E R · C O A L · C I E R A ·
· D O T A R D · Y O U V E G O T M A L I
B A Y L O R · A T A S T E · A R S E N A L
E N C O R E D · W W I · R E W · C C L
L G A · R A I S I N G T H E B R A · H E Y
A I S L E S E A T · N E O N · S R A ·
Y E T I · M U T E · A T E M · R O T C
· D P S · N E A R · I R E M E M B E R
E M S · A Q U A R T E R T O T O W · T M I
L A M · S U R · C U E · S L I P U P S
O P E N S E A · P L A S M A · A N I S E S
I L L E G A L A L I N E · B U R G L E ·
E L S O L · M A N E · I B N · L A S T
S T A T · S P E N D · A R O D · S A N E R
A R R I D · A N N I E G E T Y O U R G N U
K E A N U · C R E E P I N · E D M E E S E
S E T G O · S A R D I N E · D O O D L E D
```

9

```
C A R L S J R · H E A R T H S
A R E O L A E · O R D E R U P
N U T C A K E · O N A D I M E
A G E · M E L I K E Y · S O L
D U L Y · I B M S · C T R L
A L L E S · N E E · B L A M E
· A S S A D · G U Y L I N E R
· B Y O B · P R O P · ·
O H B O O H O O · S K O A L
N O R S K · D P T · E F L A T
E T E S · B Y E S · F O T O
M I A · C A T C H O W · H E T
I T S E A S Y · I M A W A R E
L E T S R I P · R E C R O O M
E M S P A C E · T R O Y E N S
```

10

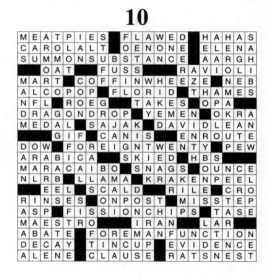

```
M E A T P I E S · F L A W E D · H A H A S
C A R O L A L T · O E N O N E · E L E N A
S U M M O N S U B S T A N C E · A A R G H
· O A T · F U S S · · R A V I O L I
M A R T · C O F F I N W H E E Z E · N E B
A L C O P O P · F L O R I D · T H A M E S
N F L · R O E G · T A K E S · O P A
D R A G O N D R O P · Y E M E N · O K R A
M E D A L · S A J A K · D A V I D L E A N
· G I F · C A N I S · E N R O U T E
D O W · F O R E I G N T W E N T Y · P E W
A R A B I C A · S K I E D · H B S ·
M A R A C A I B O · S N A G S · O U N C E
N L R B · L L A M A · K R A K E N P E E L
· E E L · S C A L D · R I L E · C R O
R I N S E S · O N P O S T · M I S S T E P
A S P · F I S S I O N C H I P S · T A S E
M A E S T R O · I R A N · L A R ·
A B A T E · F O R E M A N F U N C T I O N
D E C A Y · T I N C U P · E V I D E N C E
A L E N E · C L A U S E · R A T S N E S T
```

11

```
G R A B L E · E A S Y A C E S
R U L E O N · M O N O T O N E
I C H I N G · B R O U H A H A
P H I N D I C A T O R · L A G
P E R S O N A L A D · G E N L
E D T · N E W M E · T O S C A
· L A M E S · B R A C E S
W A V E R E D · B O I L E R S
E L E V E N · H O B B S ·
A T R I A · D I T K A · P I M
K A Y S · W I L H E L M I N A
S I M · D E S I A R N A Z J R
P R I C E C U T · R A Z Z E S
O I L L E A S E · E M D A S H
T V D I N N E R · Y E A S T Y
```

12

```
T I M E · S L I T · I C E T · C B E R
S H I E R · P A S S I N G G O · S H E R A
G A R N E R A T T E N T I O N · W E A R Y
A V A · P U R E · T K O · S E X I E R
R E C K O N S O · S E W N · D I S S I N G
P I L E · T I N T E D · C R U I S E S B Y
T E E N · T S A · S O U P · E T H A N
· P O N Y E X P R E S S · S S R
S L O M O · T R O O P · H A I · A R S
M E A N S T O · A S S · N E L L · Y E T I
L T D · G A M E T H E S Y S T E M · V O L
K I L L · F R E E · T C M · I N A F U N K
· N E E · A I L · S T O P S · T R I P E
A N N · P O P A W H E E L I E
O B E S E · B O N A · O T T · E S P Y
W A T E R G A T E · J U S T A S · T O U R
S H O T F O R · D C U P · L I P B A L M S
· N O G O O D · U N S · E L A L · E M T
A E I O U · Q U A R T E R S I Z E H A I L
P R A W N · U L U L A T I O N · W A X E N
P E N N · E L K S · S O N G · M E R E
```

13

```
J A V A S C R I P T  #  M A S S
I H A D N O I D E A  #  O N E L
M A I D E N F O R M  #  O G R E
I S O L A T E  #  #  P E T R I E
#  #  E K E  #  A P E X  #  Y A P
W S W  #  E S Q U I R E  #  B L Y
A C H E D  #  U R G E  #  P I P E
F R O M  #  M O O E D  #  T R O Y
F E D S  #  O T R O  #  P A D R E
L E A  #  E L E A N O R  #  S T D
E N T  #  R E D S  #  N E D
C I G A R S  #  #  D E T E C T O
O D I C  #  K A R A T E C H O P
N O R M  #  I C E B O X C A K E
E L L E  #  N I X O N T A P E S
```

14

```
B E T H E R E  #  G O B I G  #  T H E L A D Y
U S H E R I N  #  O H A R A  #  R E T I R E E
S Q U E A L S  #  T O N E S  #  A R I E T T A
S U R  #  S E L D O M  #  S E A D O G  #  I R R
T A B L E  #  E R N E  #  T O R E  #  E P S O N
O R E O S  #  R I T  #  U M S  #  R E T I E
P E R P  #  V O L  #  G S A  #  E S T D
#  #  G E E  #  O R E  #  N U S  #  #
H A L F F U L L  #  C H O  #  I S I T L I V E
I N P E R I L  #  Q U E R Y  #  N E M E S I S
M A N M A D E  #  U S A G E  #  A G E G A P S
#  P I E R C E  #  S A V E M E  #
I N T L  #  Y O U R M O N E Y  #  O N L Y
B R A Y E D  #  B E L A B O R  #  D R D O O M
U R N  #  S I P S  #  I T O  #  I S E E  #  G L O
T I N S T A R  #  A F T E R  #  T A X I C A B
T T Y L  #  R I F L E  #  S A T E D  #  N A T S
R A G A  #  I T O O  #  H O W E  #  A B E T
E B O N  #  S H O U L D I S T A Y  #  P I N E
S L A T  #  T E D  #  B E G  #  E R E  #  E N G R
S E T S  #  S E S  #  J L O  #  M D S  #  T S O S
```

15

```
C L A S S T R I P  #  S A L T I
L A T E T E E N S  #  A X I O M
O V E N R E A D Y  #  T E M P T
C I A  #  E M M Y  #  M O R E S O
K E M P T  #  S Y N  #  L E O
#  A C E T A T E  #  S I C S
R A L P H N A D E R  #  O G R E
O B E Y  #  C L U E S  #  C H E X
S O A R  #  H E L L O K I T T Y
A U D I  #  A N T E N N A  #
P T S  #  B I T  #  E L U D E
A T T A I N  #  D A L E  #  D E V
R H O M B  #  S A T E L L I T E
K A R E L  #  C L O S E I N O N
S T Y N E  #  H Y P E R T E X T
```

16

```
A F F O R D S  #  T A T  #  E L M O S  #  C P A
D R U M O U T  #  A G E  #  R E C A T C H A S
S A E N D R I  #  P U R I N A S T A R E O W
#  T L I E E R H E A R T E D  #  T E S L A
#  O R S O N  #  A S S  #  S E W S O N
S N I P  #  N A R C  #  T W I T  #
C A N A D A  #  O D I E  #  E L A C T P A D
A R U N U S  #  R E F  #  S T A L B O W I T E
B D I E E T T E  #  T A P I N S  #  L I B R A
S O T S  #  R E E L  #  G A L  #  S I N B A D
#  G O E S U P A N D D O W N  #
S C O W L S  #  N A P  #  A U R A  #  D A T E
O H A R A  #  D O G I E S  #  P R I M U S E G
W A R I D E A P E R  #  L I L  #  N A P I N A
S T S T E P N T  #  P I N E  #  S E E D E D
#  E A S E  #  I M A X  #  S E T S
E X H A L E  #  V A T  #  S E A M S  #
S A U N A  #  S E L F R E S T A N T E T
S C R O P M O U N T A I N  #  B R A I N R S
A T O N E O L I S  #  L P S  #  A I R C O O L
Y O N  #  L E D T O  #  L E E  #  T A L K S T O
```

17

```
P A N A M A H A T  #  P A R T B
I R O N C R O S S  #  O P E R A
G E T S A G R I P  #  T O P A Z
L A N  #  N O N S  #  D O D O
E M I T  #  S E A N  #  C A M E O
T A C O S  #  D I C K C L A R K
S P E L L S  #  D I A L  #  N S A
#  D A N K  #  S L A T  #
S S R  #  P O N S  #  E M B O S S
P H O T O B O M B  #  P A N A M
Y O U I N  #  B E L A  #  R E N E
W E L T  #  L U L U  #  S R A
A B A F T  #  S T R E T C H E R
R O D E O  #  W E A R I S O M E
E X E R T  #  F R Y O L A T O R
```

18

```
O M G  #  C L O M P S  #  P E C  #  G O R [DO]
N I L E  #  V E G O U T  #  E R R  #  O T O H
E N A C T  #  S A L Z B U R G A U S T R I A
S A M O A N  #  R E A  #  E S S E N [TI] A L
#  J U L I E A N D R E W S  #  E L O
#  P I P E T S  #  T S A  #  [LA] W S U I T
#  E D A  #  S W E D E  #  S I G M A
T H E H I L L S A R E A L I V E  #  F L A K
H O Y A  #  E L A T E  #  [SOL] V I N G T I M E
O M E N S  #  R O A C H  #  T G I
R O D G E R S A N D H A M M E R S T E I N
#  G O L  #  S I R E E  #  T I P S Y
O P E R A B U F [FA]  #  D E N C H  #  T I L E
W I N O  #  B E S T P I C T U R E O S C A R
L C D T V  #  S U S A N  #  U G H
S A S H I [MI]  #  T R I  #  A S I D E S
#  D S T  #  T H E V O N T R A P P S
T H [RE] E S O M E  #  T A N  #  A R C A N E
T H E S O U N D O F M U S I C  #  N O C A L
O R I T  #  S A X  #  R U B I E S  #  T E R M
[DO] O R S  #  A L I  #  O D E S S A  #  Y E S
```

19

```
F R O M A T O Z ■ P E E D E E
L E M O N A D E ■ L A R Y N X
I C E B O X E S ■ I T A S C A
M I L ■ N E T T L E S ■ L O M
S P E D ■ S O I L S ■ J E D I
Y E T I S ■ J E D ■ T O X I N
■ ■ V A P O R ■ V I S I N E
H O M E K E Y ■ R A G B A G S
I N A S E C ■ M U C H O ■ ■
T E X T S ■ K I T ■ T Y P E B
S O W S ■ D F L A T ■ S E M I
Q U E ■ B A C K B A Y ■ Z I P
U N B O R N ■ C A L A M I N E
A C E D I T ■ A G O N I Z E D
D E R A T E ■ P A N G R A M S
```

20

```
A C T ■ P U M A ■ P R O ■ T E A R ■ R E M
P L Y ■ E S A U ■ R E P ■ E R I E ■ A Y E
R O T T E N E G G ■ E S E ■ M A D H A T T E R
■ S C U D ■ G U I L T R I P S ■ A D D S ■
D E A R S ■ I R R I T A B L E ■ B E F O G
O S L O ■ S E S A M E S E E D S ■ L I R A
N E L S O N ■ ■ ■ ■ ■ ■ T H E R E S
S T Y ■ N E I L ■ K F C ■ H A I R ■ E S P
■ S A T E ■ R I O ■ A W L S ■
C H A T ■ K I T ■ E L M ■ P A L ■ A L P S
H O W I W I S H ■ M L I ■ P I E A S I L Y
E G O M A N I A ■ L I N ■ E T R U S C A N
C A K E D ■ L Y I N G O N ■ T O K Y O
K N E S S E T ■ A N G S T ■ P R O C E E D
S S N ■ B O A R ■ I S E E ■ D R S
■ I C O U L D C A L C U L A T E ■
A S C E N T S ■ A D A ■ S T I R S U P
M U T I N Y ■ O S M O S I S ■ R E C T O R
E R U C T ■ C R A P S H O O T ■ A R O S E
T A T T L E ■ H A R E ■ E T U I ■ D O T T E D
E L D E R ■ E N I D ■ D A T E ■ S W A Y S
```

21

```
L O B S T E R B I B ■ N S F W
A N I M A N I A C S ■ O H I O
M O N E Y T A L K S ■ R E N O
A N G E L ■ T A Y ■ S L E D
R E O ■ O M A N ■ S M E L T S
■ S R I ■ C O C A ■ G U M
W H I S T ■ E R I C B A N A
S H A M W O W ■ B A H A M E N
H A R P I S T S ■ T I R E D
O C R ■ F I S T ■ I N N ■
V A U L T S ■ P A C E ■ P R U
E M M A ■ H E T ■ W I R E S
L O P S ■ E A T E N A L I V E
E L H I ■ T H E I N S I D E R
D E S K ■ C A R T W H E E L S
```

22

```
P R O S P E C T ■ F R I S C O ■ I G A V E
H I S H O N O R ■ A U S T E N ■ O R B I T
I N L E T L I E ■ I N S U R E E N O U G H
S K O R T ■ N E A R S ■ T R Y I T ■
■ R E E F ■ Q U A C K S ■ E A T S A T
I N F I D E L C A S T R O ■ G E N O E S E
M O O ■ N I O B E ■ I N B O X S E A T S
A F L A T ■ P G A ■ S P A R T A ■ S W A T
R U I N E D ■ S T S ■ U S M C ■ A G E
I N C A N O P E N E R ■ S N O ■ O A R E D
■ I N J U R Y T A M P E R I N G ■
V E R S E ■ L I T ■ I N F I E L D G O A L
A V E ■ R A S E ■ A N O ■ L O R D L Y
N E A P ■ C A P E R S ■ Y O U ■ S O D A S
I N D U C T T A P E ■ M A Y N T ■ E M O
S L U S H I E ■ I N T A K E C O N T R O L
H Y P H E N ■ S C A R J O ■ A V E O ■
■ B S I D E ■ I E V E R ■ C R O W E
I N F A N C Y P A N T S ■ L I N K E D I N
F A R C E ■ E A R N I T ■ S N E E R I N G
S M O K Y ■ S L E E P Y ■ E G G D O N O R
```

23

```
J U M P I N J A C K F L A S H
A H O O S I E R H O L I D A Y
N O C A U S E F O R A L A R M
E H S ■ Z A P S ■ A C T S I N
■ F U N ■ I N K ■
I T E A ■ U S M ■ M A G E
O R A N G E P O P S I C L E S
T U R N E D T H E T A B L E S
A T T E N T I O N P L E A S E
S H O D ■ L T D ■ A Y E S
■ M O T ■ D S L ■
Y E S B U T ■ E D U C ■ S L O
O N E A F T E R A N O T H E R
G E T S T O F I R S T B A S E
I S T H I S S E A T T A K E N
```

24

```
W B A L E ■ F L A P ■ H A M ■ T V D A D
A I N E D ■ R O S A ■ A C E ■ B R A I S E
R O N G D R I N K S ■ S H A R E O N E S B
T L E O I I ■ G A T ■ A E N E I D ■ D A U
S A X ■ E D G I N E S S ■ T I N ■ Y O U T
B E A D E D ■ C L I M B I N G ■ O W L
S S T ■ A R E ■ M O O T ■ T M N T
■ T A N Y A ■ P O K Y ■ N C A A
T O S E L F ■ P H O N E ■ C O L D M E A L
E V E N A L I T T L E ■ B O R E ■ A V A I
T A X ■ S T R U M S ■ M A M M A L ■ A N V
O R T H ■ E A R L ■ T A S M A N I A N D E
N Y S E N A T E ■ S I C K O ■ L E S S E R
■ L A M E ■ B C C S ■ N S Y N C ■
O D E S ■ M O R K ■ A S H ■ A C T
U R N ■ T H E W A L L S ■ O O M P A H
F T E A ■ O A F ■ P E A C H P I E ■ R E D
A L S ■ P O L I S H ■ P R U ■ L E G A L I
C I S I O N T R E E ■ D I G E S T I V E A
E N U D E S ■ S R A ■ O B E Y ■ U N A F R
D E P O T ■ T A P ■ G E R E ■ P A N T Y
```

25

BIKINIWAX · OHJOY
ECONOMIZE · DUANE
DEATHSTAR · ERICA
LALO · ESL · ROLLER
AGA · STEEPEN · BOZ
MESSY · NAIL · SAVE
PROD · CARTIER
SCARUM · TEATRO
NOTEPAD · BEAR
ALOE · NAPA · CRISP
POM · LITCRIT · MIR
CRIPES · GEM · FORE
HAZED · LAXATIVES
ADEPT · OMAGAZINE
TORSO · LEMONZEST

26

TABORS · BLADES · PLICATE
ACADIA · EOLITH · RUNRIOT
STREAMINGINCA · EMBASSY
TIRO · ENZI · DESI · SLIP
EVENPAR · CASTELSEWHERE
BAT · ESE · WAR · LURID
UTTER · ADAGES · RELIEFS
DEEPSPACECANINE · MEDAL
SOIREES · TRA · SATIRE
NOTONCE · DOESIT · TOE
YOUMAKEMEWANNACASHOUT
ALF · ALETAP · ITWORKS
LATEST · DNY · CORNIER
ALEUT · REALLYBIGCASHEW
SADCASE · SAUCED · REINE
HEIDI · ILL · AGE · RTE
BACALLHANDLER · BERSERK
AVER · LENI · HILT · ALAD
LETITIA · THELIFEOFPICA
TRUSSED · TALONS · FLINTY
OYSTERS · IDOTOO · FUDGES

27

BACKSLAPS · KAGAN
OVERDIDIT · ICAME
PERISCOPE · STRAP
SRAS · KNEW · SENNA
PSIS · AMDIAL
SAGAL · SUNNY
KOALAS · PINGPONG
INTOYOU · LARAMIE
DEEPFUNK · LILACS
OLIOS · TENET
NARCOS · PEAS
OVERT · DUES · SHIN
RITAS · INTHENUDE
MERCI · SCHEDULEA
AWOKE · CHESTBUMP

28

SAJAK · HAJ · ANT · CABALS
TAHITI · EREADER · AFLCIO
ONAGER · CENTIMO · PRIMLY
WEBS · KAT · GONOW · ROGETS
ESP · BETACAM · NEWISH
RTE · INTRO · SALES · BDAY
QUOTIENT · LUST · LOUIE
TAUNTER · SADAT · SHOULDA
WHOCARES · CUPID · OUNCES
PAD · PDAS · HOLE · OPTED
CUR · GMS · NUB · KEY
FARSI · AILS · SUBJ · LAM
ROGUES · STEAD · GLOAMING
EVENBET · HEWED · ALMONDS
PERCY · HTTP · MELBLANC
SASH · LEWIS · BABYS · OBI
GROMIT · RATTERS · LOP
VALUES · NANOS · EDO · ANNO
ELAPSE · KNOCKON · GERUND
TEMPER · IINSIST · ERASES
OXEYES · ECO · NUS · RABAT

29

RAJ · ACERBIC · HEX
UTE · MADEIRA · AXE
PAT · FRANTIC · NIN
ELLS · ATTESTEDTO
ELIOTNESS · INB
NET · CEO
NOINTERESTLOANS
ALTERNATEROUTES
BEATINGARETREAT
SALESASSISTANTS
NIE · POG
ARC · PLEASESIR
RUNSACROSS · DAME
UPI · SHIATSU · TAX
ETC · CANTEEN · AGE
DOE · ANTHERS · YES

30

SWAB · GMC · RPM · RHETT
CHICA · ALOU · OUI · OEUVRE
HASAT · GUTBOMBS · PAPAYA
IMHIP · ATHENA · SPEC · PIP
NAY · HOMES · ANTIOCH · ETA
ONO · OPEN · ESCROW · ERROR
UTNE · FENCEIN · SHOUT
SAWYER · RAGA · ASP · LINTY
USER · AGER · LAG · OVEN
SPRAT · REPLETE · PAGODAS
HIE · ARAB · SFO · NENA · OLE
ICHOKED · FARMBOY · LIEGE
PEPE · ITO · OWED · AXED
LISTS · APB · MEOW · EDGARS
ACEIT · RUDOLPH · CROC
LEACH · COLONS · EBAY · TLC
ACT · ECOTAGE · BRAYS · LAO
LAM · TONE · STALER · PAYTV
ANALOG · GOTOTOWN · ELATE
NOTIPS · ERA · TOES · LOSER
DEEDS · SLR · NPR · LEIS

31

```
T R O D _ C A B O _ E F I L E
R A K E _ A N A L _ D I D O K
I C E C O L D B E V E R A G E
B E L I E V E Y O U M E _
A R Y _ D I A S _ L A P D O G
L S D _ I N N I N G _ L I N A
_ O O P _ T E A P A R T Y
E C K H A R T _ C R A C K O S
T H E C L A S H _ N E D _
R E L O _ I R O B O T _ I N S
E T Y M O N _ W O R E _ G O A
_ E L E A N O R R I G B Y
S O U N D S L I K E A P L A N
O T T O I _ A C E R _ S E L A
L O E W E _ R E M Y _ O R L Y
```

32

```
C H E A P _ M K T _ _ C H I N _ T H I G H
E A T S A L O N E _ W H A M O _ H O S E A
D I R T[YL]I N E N _ H E A R[TW]A R M I N G
E G E R _ F R E E R A N G E _ R O O S T S
_ A S T O _ T E T E _ A L B E E _
U R I _ H E E L _ S A Y I D O _ R I F T
S O M M E R _ A J A M _ N Y U K _ E N D O
A T P A R _ E B O N I E S _ A R C S I N
G O O[DN]A T U R E D _ F I N A[LN]O T I C E
E R R _ O R A L S _ S N I P _ B U N
_ S T R A Y E D _ _ P R E S S U P _
_ Q U M _ K O A N _ S A P O R _ A L F
L A U N C[HP]A R T Y _ E V E N I N[GS]T A R
A L O N S O _ R E S E E D S _ B E I G E
R O T I _ T I T I _ E S S A _ R A T O U T
D E A N _ B A A B A A _ T R E E _ N E S
_ G O R E N _ A S W E _ E A R L _
M I K A D O _ T A C O S A L A D _ A T R A
S T A T I O[NW]A G O N _ P A P E R[RT]R A I L
R O Y A L _ I R O N S _ O V E R A C T E D
P R O B E _ T A N S _ _ E A R _ G H A N A
```

33

```
S K R I L L E X _ O R D E R S
T H E D O O R S _ F O R N O W
R A D I O E R A _ F O O D I E
O K D _ T W A N G _ F O N D A
V I I I _ E N D E D _ P O R T
E S T O P _ D O N O R _ T A B
_ N R A _ S T R A T E G O
S O V I E T S _ S A M E S E X
C H O C O L A T _ G B S _
A Y N _ P A N A M _ O T T E R
P E N A _ S A L A D _ S O T S
U S E R S _ A L L O T _ M I T
L I G E T I _ Y O U R C A L L
A D U N I T _ U N B E A T E N
R O T A R Y _ P E T E R O S E
```

34

```
S U B U R B _ S C A L E D _ _ B R I D E S
A V E N U E _ O R S I N O _ G R A N I T E
G U L P E D _ L A S T D I S H E F F O R T
A L O E _ S T A V E _ L O A _ O R E S
L A W N S H A R E S _ P L A S T E R _
_ S E E K _ S H E E P T H R I L L S
B C C _ W E E K _ E T A _ E T A I L
Y O U B E T T E R W A S H O U T _ N S A
G A T E D _ H Y O I D _ P L A S M A T V
U T E S _ _ C A T S _ R A N C H O
M I X A N D M A S H _ K A R A T E S H O P
_ F O R E S T _ A L I T _ H I F I
F I N E T U N E _ T U N I C _ M E T U P
O N E _ M U S H T O M Y S U R P R I S E
A G A I N _ A I M _ T R E E _ T E D
M A R S H M A D N E S S _ L A G S _
_ O L E M I S S _ P O K E R S H I P S
R O L L _ T E N _ A Z U R E _ O K R A
S H E A F I N S P E C T O R _ N O W N O W
V I T T L E S _ I M P E N D _ D A M O N E
P O S E U R _ P U R S E S _ S K E W E D
```

35

```
G A B O R _ S O A P _ A G E D
U T E R O _ A L L O R N O N E
A R R A Y _ L E A K E D O U T
M A G N O L I A _ E M I G R E
_ G R U N T E D _ E L E C
A L G E B R A E X A M _ E S T
R O O M I E S _ S T A M P _
F L O E S _ _ K I L T S
_ G N O T E _ D U E L E R S
C P O _ N E A R E S T E X I T
H A L F _ K R A M E R S _
O N P O S T _ C U R A T O R S
M E L S D I N E R _ C O V E T
P R E S S T I M E _ K N E E D
S A X E _ E M E R _ S E R F S
```

36

```
B E A K S _ S H Y E R _ S A H A R A
O X L I P _ T I M M A R A _ O P E N E R S
B E T S Y _ A N O O K O F T H E N O R T H
S C A M _ A M O K _ S I T I N S _ M A I A
_ R E D L I N E S _ C E C E _ B A T E D
E A R T O O N E S H E A R T _ B A L E R S
A R A _ N A G _ P O L _ A D A N O
S E I Z E D _ O R M A N C O N Q U E S T
Y A L E U _ P E T E _ C O S T _ U S A I R
_ A P G A R _ S T U _ T I O _ R T E
C O W L _ A R R O W M I N D E D _ A P E X
A H A _ C P A _ A A A _ A D A G E
P H Y L A _ B A H T _ M U N I _ C R E E P
O I S E P O L L U T I O N _ B L O N D E
_ V O W E L _ M T M _ D R E _ D E E
H A M I T E _ I C E P I E C E O F W O R K
O B O T E _ I S O N _ F R A C A S E S
M O N T _ B H O P A L _ I P O D _ S P O T
E U R O T R A N S M I T T E R _ A L E V E
S N O W C A T _ T E A S E R S _ C E R E S
_ D E N U D E _ O L O R D _ H Y M N S
```

37

```
M U F F I N T O P ■ K E B A B
O N E I N F O U R ■ I V A N A
A S I F I C A R E ■ N O T I N
T E N E T ■ ■ S P Y G L A S S
E A T D I R T ■ S U T U R E ■
D T S ■ A E O N ■ M U T A T E
■ ■ P L A Y A T ■ T I N T S
A G H A ■ M E T O O ■ O G E E
N O U N S ■ D A R W I N ■ ■
Y E N T A S ■ L U I S ■ F A R
■ S K Y L A B ■ S E A H A R E
A G E L I M I T ■ D U T C H
M A R I N ■ D O C T O R W H O
A G E N A ■ E N T E R T A I N
H A D E S ■ T E N N E S S E E
```

38

```
T K T ■ O V U M ■ V A C ■ R O P E W A Y
U N H ■ N A N O ■ D E N Y ■ A T E D I R T
L E E ■ C U C A M O N G A ■ G O G G L E D
I L L T E L L ■ O F T E N ■ L I L ■ ■
P L O Y ■ T E A R F U L ■ G R E E N I N G
■ C P A ■ A N T ■ R O L L I N G G A I T
G R U E L I N G ■ M A S T I F F ■ M N O
R E S O L D ■ E W E ■ S A L I E N C E S
A C T ■ A L B R I G H T ■ E N D E A R
B U T C H E R E D ■ Y A O ■ O A R ■
■ R R R ■ B R O K E N R I B ■ T L C
E O S ■ W I N ■ B R A N C H O F F ■ S L R
B E C O M E ■ N A T I O N A L ■ ■
P R I S C I L L A ■ C T N ■ N O R W A Y
I O N ■ D I A G R A M ■ E G G W H I T E
L I F E I S S W E E T ■ P R O ■ N E L
E L L I O T T S ■ M A Y I S E E ■ I L L S
■ O D D ■ D O N U T ■ S P A N I E L
R E W E A V E ■ O V E R A G A I N ■ A A A
E X E R T E D ■ R E N T ■ S P C A ■ M S N
C O R S E T S ■ A D D ■ T E S T ■ S E T
```

39

```
D R I P P O T ■ B E A T S M E
R E M O R S E ■ U P D A T E D
U P P S A L A ■ L E A K I N G
G R O T T O ■ C L E M E N T E
C I R C E ■ S L Y ■ S U G A R
Z E T A ■ A L O F T ■ P O L S
A V E R A G E S O U T ■ ■
R E D D I A P E R B A B I E S
■ ■ L I T T H E T O R C H
A S T I ■ N A R I S ■ N O O R
S P A N G ■ R O M ■ P E N N I
H I N D U G O D ■ W E S S O N
A N G E L O U ■ T I T M I C E
R E L E A R N ■ O N R A D A R
P L E D G E D ■ M O O N E R S
```

40

```
B R E A D S ■ R O M A ■ O D D S ■ S T E M
M A R I N E C O R P S ■ K E E P S C O O L
W I N D A W A T C H A P L A Y A P R A N K
■ N O E L ■ T I A ■ T H A N ■ R O A D S
■ ■ A M E N ■ H E E ■ S T O W ■ ■
T H U M B A R I D E A W A V E A F L A G
L E S S O ■ R P M ■ E E L ■ T U G
C R E D ■ F L A T ■ C R I M E S C E N E
■ D O A F L I P A C O I N A P H R A S E
■ S N O O Z E ■ H U E S ■ S E T S I N
M T M ■ N O W ■ S I P ■ B O A ■ E T A
A R A R A T ■ S A L E ■ C H A N T S
R U N A L I G H T A F I R E A S H O T
C I T Y S T R E E T ■ S U M S ■ R U L E
S S R ■ A B A ■ S A M ■ B A T B O Y
M A K E A C A T C H A B U S A T A B L E
■ A C N E ■ A R K ■ P A D S ■ ■
W O R L D ■ A G R I ■ A L B ■ T O O L
F I L E A R E T U R N A B O O K A T R I P
T V A N T E N N A ■ K A R A T E K I C K S
D E F S ■ A T O M ■ S H A D ■ Y E S S E S
```

41

```
H A T C H E T J O B ■ M F A S
Y E A H I M S U R E ■ A R G O
E S K I M O K I S S ■ N E O N
N O E L ■ ■ S C O T C H E G G
A P I E C E ■ E N B L O C ■
■ ■ A H A S ■ Y O U L I E
S C E N E S H O P ■ W R I S T
T O X ■ S T O O D O N ■ M T S
E D I T H ■ O F F I C E B O Y
M A T H I S ■ ■ S N A G ■
■ ■ L E R N E R ■ K R O N O R
P L A C E A B E T ■ ■ T U N A
R E N U ■ R O C K G A R D E N
O V E R ■ F L O O D L I G H T
W I S E ■ S A N D P A P E R S
```

42

```
J U S T ■ A L U M ■ M B A ■ H O T D A T E S
U H A U L ■ T E R A ■ O O H ■ A T H E N I A N
L U I G I ■ S T U D F A R M ■ G R E W I N T O
E R N ■ S T E T ■ S O N N E T ■ A L S O ■
S A T ■ T H A I ■ E R S T ■ E S S O ■ N Y R O
F U S E ■ N O N O ■ O N K P ■ N O S O A P
C O R E ■ N I G H ■ N A B E ■ E G G S ■ U D E
S H A Y ■ E R O O ■ E D E R ■ C O K E ■ K I N
P A N S ■ W O N K Y ■ E M O ■ I R I S ■ N A B
O R C ■ D Y N E ■ A L L Y ■ W A G S ■ R O T A
T A I ■ R A Y S ■ W E E B ■ A L E S ■ E W E R
■ S V E N ■ H E L M ■ A C D C ■ G N A W ■
T A C O ■ K C A R ■ O N B Y ■ O T O E ■ H E F
A R O W ■ E R I S ■ N A Y S ■ U H O H ■ A X L
G E L ■ J E E R ■ O S H ■ T I R E D ■ E T U I
S A L ■ O W E D ■ A Q U A ■ S T U N ■ W I D E
A W E ■ K O K O ■ T U M S ■ O M N I ■ A M E S
L A G G E R ■ W I S E ■ P I N A ■ G I N S
E Y E S ■ K E N S ■ E R I N ■ R A H M ■ A T V
■ H A S P ■ H A Z A R D ■ T I T O ■ Y E E
M A R A T H O N ■ H E R E I T I S ■ F R I A R
O V E R R O D E ■ E R I ■ G O A L ■ F A N O N
B A G P I P E S ■ M S N ■ O G L E ■ O G R E
```

43

```
KIDSMEAL■FRAMED
EMINENCE■LADYDI
DUXELLES■ICONIC
SPIRE■ATANYRATE
■FETE■WEST■ASHY
ROC■SNARLSAT■■
ERRS■ORS■TWISTS
DIAMOND■BOLOTIE
OTTERS■RAN■NAME
■LETTUCES■TED
IDOL■ASST■HIES
DONTERASE■INLAW
INSERT■ERUPTIVE
ONESIE■LISTENED
MATTER■LABORERS
```

44

```
TACO■TEACH■PILLS■ARF
ALBUM■WANDA■INDIA■DEL
ITSNOWONDER■LOFTY■IOU
■TRESS■KRONA■SKORT
TAMER■PROFIT■IRONAGE
CIRCLE■RABID■RTE■ENS
AMOK■GOTON■SUHWEET
SEMIANNUAL■TOMFOOLERY
TRANSFAT■COLOURS■NOI
■LILT■SEAWORLD■SNAP
ANDES■KELVINS■QUADS
TORY■HOARSENS■NOUN
OVO■DECRIED■VANISHED
MAPLELEAFS■SMARTPHONE
■DEFEATS■ROOMY■IMAC
NOV■NNE■LAPUP■STNICK
PAWEDAT■SENSEI■TWEET
ASNER■RELIC■ROUES
PAM■ALEXA■HIBERNATION
ALE■WINIT■EKEBY■KASHI
SSN■SECTS■RELAX■TOMB
```

45

```
■INTS■EVILQUEEN
OMOUT■MADEAPLAY
WEIRE■ISLANDERS
ENGRET■TENTACLE
■SHORAGE■SAT■
■STOIST■SEVEN
PRISONRTH■DIVA
AOK■FYI■EWE■BEG
DUES■OFMASTERS
STAIR■TRAITE
■LIB■ENTRADA
TELEPORT■SERING
IRONSTONE■AMODE
TICTACTOE■TORRO
SNOWWHITE■SNEE
```

46

```
■UPC■ASIS■IMPACT■SODS
STEADIEST■GUITAR■UNIT
EARLYLEAD■AFLAME■REDA
PHILS■YOST■FADINGFAST
■ALPO■WOLF■CLEFTS
ONTHEOUTSIDE■COHORT
ICEAXE■SACS■FORA■ERA
SOMNI■ROSE■BARONS■RET
ESP■CLOTH■BACKSTRETCH
■OBSESS■AUST■ACHOO
GURU■GAINSGROUND■HENS
OHARA■OKLA■VOODOO
TURNFORHOME■KUDZU■TSP
TRY■LYSINE■KALE■TOHOE
OAT■ETES■TUNA■ACCENT
■ABACUS■MAKESACHARGE
VOTENO■VAIL■SKOR■
INTHEMONEY■AITS■VIOLA
ALOE■OBERON■BYALENGTH
LAOS■VIAGRA■MCDONALDS
SYST■ATREST■SOSA■SES
```

47

```
ZEROWASTE■YUCCA
EXOTICPET■OBOES
TAXISQUAD■DARES
AMYS■URN■HANDLE
■FINERY■GOOS■
HAMLET■COATING■
ONAIR■SKATE■BRB
UNIBROW■STANLEE
RON■EXIST■SPEED
■DESTINY■RERUNS
DOVE■DENVER■
EMERGE■CIG■WAGE
RINGO■SHRINKRAY
ENTER■ARTFORGER
KISSY■SOUTHPOLE
```

48

```
ONPAPER■CHATS■ALCAPP
FAILURE■OILRIG■DAUBED
FIGHTINJUSTICE■ITSPAT
AVIA■KEELS■TKT■PESOS
LETIT■GED■ROOST■PASHA
■GENERALINFORMATION
MOL■ECO■AMS■VOUS■TOG
BRAININJURY■JETES■ITE
ADONIS■EPA■EROS■AVER
SOSAD■SLIPON■ULSTERS
■COURTINJUNCTION
EQUALTO■NESTER■LOOPY
LUNN■MARK■FRA■TOOKTO
RAS■HOSES■SISTERINLAW
ODU■ESTD■APT■YOS■ASS
PRIVATEINVESTMENTS
OUTED■DREAD■HOB■SIGMA
■PARCH■EUR■LAMAR■POOR
LEBEAU■CRIMINALINTENT
IDLEST■TOCOME■LAYETTE
USENET■NEONS■SLEAZES
```

49

W	I	N	A	T	L	I	F	E	■	T	A	R	T	H
A	M	I	N	O	A	C	I	D	■	A	W	A	R	E
S	P	A	N	D	R	E	L	S	■	P	E	C	A	N
S	O	G	■	O	V	A	L	■	E	A	S	E	I	N
U	S	A	F	■	A	X	I	O	M	S	■	C	P	A
P	E	R	I	L	■	E	N	D	O	■	R	A	S	E
■	S	A	L	A	D	■	G	E	N	D	E	R	E	D
■	■	I	R	A	Q	■	S	E	R	B	■			
S	T	E	A	K	R	U	B	■	Y	I	E	L	D	
T	E	A	L	■	W	A	I	L	■	P	L	E	A	S
J	A	G	■	F	I	D	G	E	T	■	S	A	N	E
O	R	E	G	O	N	■	P	A	R	K	■	V	I	C
H	O	R	U	S	■	H	A	V	E	A	B	E	E	R
N	U	L	L	S	■	O	P	E	N	T	A	B	L	E
S	T	Y	L	E	■	P	I	N	T	E	R	E	S	T

50

I	S	I	S	■	T	E	S	T	S	■	O	T	O	H	■	S	T	A	M	P
D	U	N	E	■	E	R	N	I	E	■	H	E	R	O	■	E	A	S	Y	A
A	G	F	A	■	S	I	L	E	X	■	M	E	N	U	■	G	E	H	R	Y
■	A	L	L	E	L	E	■	S	O	B	■	P	O	S	T	A	■	B	I	O
T	R	U	E	F	A	■	H	O	L	Y	W	A	T	E	R	■	R	I	A	L
A	L	E	R	T	■	D	E	N	O	T	E	D	■	B	E	L	I	N	D	A
C	O	N	S	■	O	E	D	■	G	E	T	■	S	O	N	I	C	■		
T	A	Z	■	N	G	S	D	A	Y	■	S	E	A	T	B	E	L	T	S	
■	F	A	M	I	L	I	A	L	■	S	P	E	C	T	■	S	C	I	O	N
■	■	E	K	E	S	■	D	R	E	A	M	T	■		■	A	E	R	O	
T	H	R	E	E	■	T	H	E	A	R	T	I	S	T	■	O	K	N	O	W
R	O	O	T	■	I	N	S	T	E	P	■	H	A	T	E	■				
I	S	A	I	D	■	I	N	T	H	A	■	R	E	A	L	I	S	T	S	
P	E	N	N	Y	A	N	T	E	■	H	O	W	W	A	S	■	E	T	C	
■	G	A	U	S	S	■	P	G	A	■	E	E	N	■	P	A	I	L		
E	D	M	U	N	D	I	■	B	A	R	N	A	R	D	■	S	O	T	T	O
S	E	E	P	■	I	D	L	E	H	A	N	D	S	■	A	L	L	A	C	Y
T	A	R	■	O	T	I	O	N	■	M	I	R	■	A	F	R	E	S	H	
O	N	E	P	M	■	O	U	S	T	■	B	E	A	L	L	■	A	T	I	T
P	I	S	A	N	■	U	P	O	N	■	A	N	I	T	A	■	X	E	N	A
S	E	T	S	I	■	S	E	N	T	■	L	O	G	I	C	■	E	R	G	O

The New York Times

Crossword Puzzles

The #1 Name in Crosswords

Available at your local bookstore or online at nytimes.com/nytstore

Coming Soon!

Holiday Spirit Crosswords	978-1-250-07539-0
Large-Print Train Your Brain Crossword Puzzles	978-1-250-07545-1
Rainy Day Crosswords	978-1-250-07541-3
Sunday Crossword Puzzles, Volume 41	978-1-250-07544-4
Thrilling Thursday Crosswords	978-1-250-07543-7
Tons of Puns Crosswords	978-1-250-07540-6
Will Shortz's Favorite Puzzlemakers	978-1-250-03255-3
Wonderful Wednesday Crosswords	978-1-250-07542-0
Best of Friday Crosswords	978-1-250-05590-3
Best of Saturday Crosswords	978-1-250-05591-0
Easy as Pie Crosswords	978-1-250-05592-7
Piece of Cake Puzzles	978-1-250-05594-1
Coffee Shop Crosswords	978-1-250-06336-6
Cup of Tea and Crosswords	978-1-250-06333-5
Extra Easy Crosswords	978-1-250-06338-0
Marvelous Monday Crosswords	978-1-250-06339-7
Terrific Tuesday Crosswords	978-1-250-06340-3

Special Editions

'Tis the Season Crosswords	978-1-250-05589-7
Will Shortz Presents The Crossword Bible	978-1-250-06335-9
Winter Wonderland Crosswords	978-1-250-03919-4
Pocket-Size Puzzles: Crosswords	978-1-250-03915-6
Will Shortz Picks His Favorite Puzzles	978-0-312-64550-2
Crosswords for the Holidays	978-0-312-64544-1
Crossword Lovers Only: Easy Puzzles	978-0-312-54619-9
Crossword Lovers Only: Easy to Hard Puzzles	978-0-312-68139-5
Little Black & White Book of Holiday Crosswords	978-0-312-65424-5
Little Black (and White) Book of Sunday Crosswords	978-0-312-59003-1
Will Shortz's Wittiest, Wackiest Crosswords	978-0-312-59034-5
Crosswords to Keep Your Brain Young	978-0-312-37658-8
Little Black (and White) Book of Crosswords	978-0-312-36105-1
Will Shortz's Favorite Crossword Puzzles	978-0-312-30613-7
Will Shortz Presents Crosswords for 365 Days	978-0-312-36121-1

Easy Crosswords

Easy Crossword Puzzles Volume 15	978-1-250-04486-0
Easy Crossword Puzzles Volume 16	978-1-250-06337-3
Volumes 2–14 also available	

Tough Crosswords

Tough Crossword Puzzles Vol. 13	978-0-312-34240-3
Tough Crossword Puzzles Vol. 12	978-0-312-32442-1
Volumes 9–11 also available	

Sunday Crosswords

Snowed-In Sunday Crosswords	978-1-250-05595-8
Sunday Crossword Puzzles Volume 40	978-1-250-05596-5
Smart Sunday Crosswords Volume 1	978-1-250-06341-0

Sweetheart Sunday Crosswords	978-1-250-06334-2
Sweet Sunday Crosswords	978-1-250-01592-6
Sunday Crossword Puzzles Volume 38	978-1-250-01544-0
Sunday in the Surf Crosswords	978-1-250-00924-1
Simply Sundays	978-1-250-00390-4
Fireside Sunday Crosswords	978-0-312-64546-5
Snuggle Up Sunday Crosswords	978-0-312-59057-4
Stay in Bed Sunday Crosswords	978-0-312-68144-9
Relaxing Sunday Crosswords	978-0-312-65429-0
Finally Sunday Crosswords	978-0-312-64113-9
Crosswords for a Lazy Sunday	978-0-312-60820-0
Sunday's Best	978-0-312-37637-5
Sunday at Home Crosswords	978-0-312-37834-3

Omnibus

More Monday Crossword Puzzles Omnibus Vol. 2	978-1-250-04493-8
More Tuesday Crossword Puzzles Omnibus Vol. 2	978-1-250-04494-5
Monday Crossword Puzzle Omnibus	978-1-250-02523-4
Tuesday Crossword Puzzle Omnibus	978-1-250-02526-5
Crossword Puzzle Omnibus Vol. 16	978-0-312-36104-1
Sunday Crossword Omnibus Vol. 10	978-0-312-59006-2
Easy Crossword Puzzles Omnibus Volume 10	978-1-250-04924-7
Previous volumes also available	

Portable Size Format

Will Shortz Presents A Year of Crosswords	978-1-250-04487-7
Curious Crosswords	978-1-250-04488-4
Bedside Crosswords	978-1-250-04490-7
Crosswords to Supercharge Your Brainpower	978-1-250-04491-4
Best of Sunday Crosswords	978-1-250-04492-1
Teatime Crosswords	978-1-250-04489-1
Soothing Sunday Crosswords	978-1-250-03917-0
Best of Wednesday Crosswords	978-1-250-03913-2
Best of Thursday Crosswords	978-1-250-03912-5
Sunday Crossword Puzzles Volume 39	978-1-250-03918-7
Will Shortz Wants You to Solve Crosswords!	978-1-250-04918-6
Crosswords to Start Your Day	978-1-250-04919-3
Crosswords For Your Commute	978-1-250-04923-0
Easy Does It Crosswords	978-1-250-04920-9
Relax and Unwind Crosswords	978-1-250-03254-6
Smart Sunday Crosswords	978-1-250-03253-9
Homestyle Crosswords	978-1-250-01543-3
Picnic Blanket Crosswords	978-1-250-00391-1
Huge Book of Easy Crosswords	978-1-250-00399-7
Keep Calm and Crossword On	978-0-312-68141-8
Best of Monday Crosswords	978-1-250-00926-5
Best of Tuesday Crosswords	978-1-250-00927-2
Mad About Crosswords	978-1-250-00923-4
All the Crosswords That Are Fit to Print	978-1-250-00925-8
For the Love of Crosswords	978-1-250-02522-7
Sweet and Simple Crosswords	978-1-250-02525-8
Surrender to Sunday Crosswords	978-1-250-02524-1
Easiest Crosswords	978-1-250-02519-7
Will's Best	978-1-250-02531-9
Other volumes also available	

St. Martin's Griffin